Collaboration and the Future of Education

Current educational reforms have given rise to various types of "educational Taylorism," which encourage the creation of efficiency models in pursuit of a unified way to teach. In history education curricula, this has been introduced through scripted textbook-based programs such as Teachers' Curriculum Institute's *History Alive!* and completely online curricula. They include the jargon of authentic methods, such as primary sources, cooperative learning, differentiated instruction, and access to technology; yet the craft of teaching is removed, and an experience that should be marked by discovery and reflection is replaced with comparatively empty processes.

This volume provides systematic models and examples of ways that history teachers can compete with and effectively halt this transformation. The alternatives the authors present are based on collaborative models that address the art of teaching for pre-service and practicing secondary history teachers as well as collegiate history educators. Relying on original research and a maturing body of secondary literature on historical thinking, this book illuminates how collaboration can create real historical learning.

Gordon P. Andrews is associate professor of history at Grand Valley State University, USA.

Wilson J. Warren is professor of history at Western Michigan University, USA.

James P. Cousins is director of undergraduate studies and master faculty specialist at Western Michigan University, USA.

Routledge Research in Education

For a full list of titles in this series, please visit www.routledge.com

129 **The Age of STEM**
Educational policy and practice
across the world in Science,
Technology, Engineering
and Mathematics
*Edited by Brigid Freeman, Simon
Marginson and Russell Tytler*

130 **Mainstreams, Margins
and the Spaces In-between**
New possibilities for
education research
*Edited by Karen Trimmer,
Ali Black and Stewart Riddle*

131 **Arts-based and Contemplative
Practices in Research
and Teaching**
Honoring Presence
*Edited by Susan Walsh,
Barbara Bickel, and Carl Leggo*

132 **Interrogating Critical Pedagogy**
The Voices of Educators of Color
in the Movement
*Edited by Pierre Wilbert Orelus
and Rochelle Brock*

133 **My School**
Listening to parents, teachers and
students from a disadvantaged
educational setting
Lesley Scanlon

134 **Education, Nature, and Society**
Stephen Gough

135 **Learning Technologies
and the Body**
Integration and Implementation
In Formal and Informal
Learning Environments
Edited by Victor Lee

136 **Landscapes of Specific
Literacies in Contemporary
Society**
Exploring a social model
of literacy
*Edited by Vicky Duckworth
and Gordon Ade-Ojo*

137 **The Education of Radical
Democracy**
Sarah S. Amsler

138 **Aristotelian Character Education**
Kristján Kristjánsson

139 **Performing Kamishibai**
Tara McGowan

140 **Educating Adolescent Girls
Around the Globe**
*Edited by Sandra L. Stacki
and Supriya Baily*

141 **Quality Teaching and the
Capability Approach**
Evaluating the work and
governance of women teachers
in rurual Sub-Saharan Africa
Alison Buckler

142 **Using Narrative Inquiry for Educational Research in the Asia Pacific**
Edited by Sheila Trahar and Wai Ming Yu

143 **The Hidden Role of Software in Educational Research**
Policy to Practice
By Tom Liam Lynch

144 **Education, Leadership and Islam**
Theories, discourses and practices from an Islamic perspective
Saeeda Shah

145 **English Language Teacher Education in Chile**
A cultural historical activity theory perspective
Malba Barahona

146 **Navigating Model Minority Stereotypes**
Asian Indian Youth in South Asian Diaspora
Rupam Saran

147 **Evidence-based Practice in Education**
Functions of evidence and causal presuppositions
Tone Kvernbekk

148 **A New Vision of Liberal Education**
The good of the unexamined life
Alistair Miller

149 **Transatlantic Reflections on the Practice-Based PhD in Fine Art**
Jessica B. Schwarzenbach and Paul M. W. Hackett

150 **Drama and Social Justice**
Theory, research and practice in international contexts
Edited by Kelly Freebody and Michael Finneran

151 **Education, Identity and Women Religious, 1800–1950**
Convents, classrooms and colleges
Edited by Deirdre Raftery and Elizabeth Smyth

152 **School Health Education in Changing Times**
Curriculum, pedagogies and partnerships
Deana Leahy, Lisette Burrows, Louise McCuaig, Jan Wright and Dawn Penney

153 **Progressive Sexuality Education**
The Conceits of Secularism
Mary Lou Rasmussen

154 **Collaboration and the Future of Education**
Preserving the Right to Think and Teach Historically
Gordon Andrews, Warren J. Wilson, and James Cousins

155 **Theorizing Pedagogical Interaction**
Insights from Conversation Analysis
Hansun Zhang Waring

156 **Interdisciplinary Approaches to Distance Teaching**
Connected Classrooms in Theory and Practice
Alan Blackstock and Nathan Straight

156 **How Arts Education Makes a Difference**
Research examining successful classroom practice and pedagogy
Edited by Josephine Fleming, Robyn Gibson and Michael Anderson

157 **Populism, Media and Education**
Challenging discrimination in contemporary digital societies
Edited by Maria Ranieri

Collaboration and the Future of Education

Preserving the Right to Think and Teach Historically

Gordon P. Andrews
Wilson J. Warren
James P. Cousins

NEW YORK AND LONDON

First published 2016
by Routledge
711 Third Avenue, New York, NY 10017

and by Routledge
2 Park Square, Milton Park, Abingdon, Oxon OX14 4RN

Routledge is an imprint of the Taylor & Francis Group, an informa business

© 2016 Taylor & Francis

The right of Gordon Andrews, Warren J. Wilson, and James Cousins to be identified as author of this work has been asserted by them in accordance with sections 77 and 78 of the Copyright, Designs and Patents Act 1988.

All rights reserved. No part of this book may be reprinted or reproduced or utilised in any form or by any electronic, mechanical, or other means, now known or hereafter invented, including photocopying and recording, or in any information storage or retrieval system, without permission in writing from the publishers.

Trademark Notice: Product or corporate names may be trademarks or registered trademarks, and are used only for identification and explanation without intent to infringe.

Library of Congress Cataloging-in-Publication Data
CIP data has been applied for.

ISBN: 978-0-415-73439-4 (hbk)
ISBN: 978-1-315-83262-3 (ebk)

Typeset in Sabon
by Apex CoVantage, LLC

Printed and bound in the United States of America by Publishers Graphics, LLC on sustainably sourced paper.

Contents

Acknowledgments		ix
1	Introduction	1

PART I
The Current Landscape of History Education

2	*History Alive!* Is History Dead: Problems with Textbook-Driven Instruction	11
3	The Teaching American History Project: Teachers' Assessments of Its Classroom Connection	22
4	Crossing the Educational Rubicon: Collaboration as a Model for Change	31

PART II
The Argument for Creating the Space to Think and Teach Historically

5	Developing a Craft Approach to Teaching History: What We Can Learn from the Gilder Lehrman Institute of American History's National History Teachers of the Year	47
6	A Collaborative Model for Assessing Teachers: Why We Need It	58

viii *Contents*

PART III
Collaborating to Create Authentic Historical Thinking and Learning

7 Historiography in High School Classrooms: A Review
   of the Literature   75

8 Lifting the Veil: Teachers and Historiography   87

9 Students and Historiography: How Collaboration
   Improves Learning   97

10 Collaboration and Pre-Service Teachers: Using Historiography
    as Pedagogy   109

11 Alternative Education: Historiography and Historical
    Thinking in the Nontraditional Classroom   119

    Afterword   127
    Index   129

Acknowledgments

The authors gratefully acknowledge the work and spirit of collaboration expressed by the elementary and secondary teachers they have worked with over the past many years. In particular, we are immensely grateful to the efforts of Eric Alburtus, Kent Baker, Sara Brown, Sue Hoffman, Patricia Johnson, and Tama Salisbury at Portage (Michigan) Central High School and Terry Butcher at Barclay Hills Educational Center and the Climax-Scotts Adult Alternative Education Program. Without their great sacrifices in time and energy to participate in our collaborative endeavors, there would be no story to tell here.

The authors also thank *The History Teacher* for allowing us permission to use "Crossing the Educational Rubicon without the TAH: Collaboration among University and Secondary-Level History Educators" as chapter 4, and *Teaching History: A Journal of Methods* for allowing us permission to use "Developing a Craft Approach in History Teaching: What We Can Learn from the Gilder Lehrman Institute of American History's National Teachers of the Year" for chapter 5 in this book.

1 Introduction

Passage and implementation of the No Child Left Behind Act has accelerated the trend toward the replacement of craft methods of teaching with various types of "educational Taylorism." As used in this book, educational Taylorism refers to the use of commercially–or institutionally–developed scripts, aids, texts, or methods that replace the accumulated experience and wisdom associated with teacher-scholars. Raymond E. Callahan's seminal study of how Taylorism impacted schools, published in 1962, focused primarily on how administrators adopted various business practices. He explains how school superintendents in particular espoused cost accounting procedures that by the 1920s affected class size and teaching loads.[1] However, the application of Taylorism to classroom teaching practices was not yet common practice when Callahan's book was published. But in more recent years, educational Taylorism has encouraged the creation of efficiency models in the pursuit of "the one best way" to teach.[2] Jonathan Rees, for instance, has asserted that "[s]cientific management in the classroom does not respect the idea that teachers know what to teach their students or how best to teach it."[3] Adherents of educational Taylorism, wittingly or not, are now moving aggressively and regrettably in the direction of telling teachers exactly what and how to teach, resulting in the erosion of authentic craft methods of teaching, particularly at the elementary and secondary school levels.

Schools have introduced educational Taylorism in many ways, but arguably the most common forms have been in thoroughly scripted textbook-based programs or in "blended" or completely online curricula. Regarding the former, Teachers' Curriculum Institute's *History Alive!* is a very popular program that provides teachers with access to resources they would otherwise lack, such as primary sources, scripted simulations (historical and geographic), and photos.[4] Because it enhances their products' popularity with administrators, publishers routinely guarantee school districts that all lessons will be benchmarked to state standards.[5] Teachers are presented lessons in a step-by-step process, involving worksheets, popcorn reading, drawing and coloring historical figures or concepts, and discussing vocabulary or events that rarely move beyond the knowledge level, let alone require

2 Introduction

students to think historically in ways that historians might deem genuine or authentic.[6]

Technology-based curricula currently include "blended" or "hybrid" models, or in some cases total online learning. Blended models usually involve two types of experiences. One type is a three-day rotation for which the teacher is literally handed a script to read to students on the first day, followed by two days during which students work in groups answering an "essential" question by assembling a five-panel PowerPoint.[7] Another form of blended curriculum makes use of technology offering students the "opportunity" to learn at home and at school. These programs require students to work from home two or three days a week and attend a traditional class two or three days a week, depending on the district.[8] Much has been made in educational circles recently about "flipped" classrooms in which students are presented with content outside of class time, usually via videos or lectures online, and then asked to work on application problems during class time. However, as with other blended models, the online component is often scripted in a way that may not be under the classroom instructor's direct control.[9]

Quite often the online models remove the teacher from crucial parts of the learning process, and as such, the teacher is transferred into a facilitator of large numbers of students engaged in basic knowledge-gathering and -retention activities. Students read online texts and lectures and then test until they reach the compulsory percentage to pass the chapter. These new curricula include the jargon of authentic methods, such as primary sources, cooperative learning, differentiated instruction, and access to technology. The problem is that the craft of teaching is removed in whole or in part and increasingly, replaced with a process that unfortunately has only the thin veneer of authentic history teaching and learning associated with it. Particularly depressing about this trend is that pre-service teachers are also trained to use the same processes at the expense of learning traditional craft approaches. An experience that should be marked by discovery and reflection is replaced with comparatively empty processes.[10]

Many public and private groups and movements can be blamed for the growth of educational Taylorism. But the crucial issue is: What can be done to combat it? This book provides systematic examples of ways teachers can compete with or perhaps, effectively stymie this transformation in the field of history instruction and learning. The alternatives presented in this book are based on collaborative models that address the craft of teaching for pre-service and practicing secondary history teachers, which also have implications for collegiate history educators. Relying on original research and a maturing body of secondary literature on historical thinking, this book illuminates how collaboration can improve historical thinking and learning.

Most of the book's examples and related discussion are grounded in the more than decade-long relationships among teachers and students at Portage (Michigan) Central High School (PCHS), Western Michigan University

Introduction 3

(WMU), and, more recently, Grand Valley State University (GVSU).[11] The relationships that developed in the exercise of individual agency among teachers and students provide the basis for substantive reform and demonstrate the possibilities that lie within the reach of teachers and schools nationwide to develop genuine historical learning processes. This book's premise is that collaboration needs to be grounded in local relationships among professors, classroom teachers, and pre-collegiate and collegiate students.[12] Once teachers are given the freedom to engage their students in authentic historical exercises, then products and processes associated with educational Taylorism need not become albatrosses.

The book is organized into three sections. Part I highlights both obstacles to more authentic use of craft-based teaching models and existing efforts that have partly addressed these obstacles. Chapter 2 focuses on one of the most significant obstacles to authentic history teaching and learning: teachers' overreliance on textbooks. Of course, the driving force behind textbook dependence is not simply teachers' decisions; it is integrally related to the changing landscape of education nationwide that for more than a generation has been driven by accountability and assessment concerns. Nevertheless, the chapter argues that even textbooks that purport to use the best models of instructional theory and practice and provide teachers with crucial content support are no substitutes for teachers' disciplinary knowledge and skills.

Chapter 3 provides insights into K–12 classroom teachers' concerns with current history teaching practices by examining a longstanding Teaching American History (TAH) project's efforts to provide instructional guidance for teachers in southwest Michigan between 2004 and 2012. Based on observation and survey data, the chapter highlights not only teachers' concerns but also features of the collaborative nature of the TAH project that were valuable. Although the TAH project no longer exists, understanding its contributions is valuable in helping future collaborative efforts in the field of history.

Chapter 4 explains another project—involving the K–12 and academic partners who are the primary constituents described in the book's Part III—that illuminates how collaboration impacted the various instructors and students at both the collegiate and high school levels. This chapter provides a baseline of understanding the dimensions of collaboration that infuse other parts of the book.

Part II highlights two important dimensions of craft-based teaching models as applied to history instruction and teacher evaluation. Chapter 5 explains how craft models of teaching are reflected in the criteria used to determine the Gilder Lehrman Institute of American History's National History Teachers of the Year (HTOY) award winners. The award acknowledges a distinctive group of teachers who eschew a process approach and instead, actively pursue their careers using a craft approach. Collectively, these elementary and secondary teachers share a disposition about the

4 *Introduction*

teaching of history that provides insightful solutions to some of the most pressing problems facing history education. Based on interviews with several of these teachers, this chapter explores how they developed and implemented their craft, how they saw the connections between teacher training and in-service development, and how a craft approach advances historical thinking. It also provides insights into the vexing problem of evaluating what good history teaching is. These teachers emphasize how nurturing the craft of history teaching is vital to the future practice of teaching and learning for all students.

Chapter 6 explores the elements of a craft-based, collaborative model of teacher evaluation also based on the Gilder Lehrman Institute of American History's HTOY award. Assessment has long been a stress point for history teachers, particularly when they are evaluated by administrators who view history education as a process rather than as a fundamental part of a craft approach. New research involving the HTOY program provides insights into the collaborative model used by the Gilder Lehrman Institute of American History to determine its national winner and what can be learned from that process. A unique element of the Gilder Lehrman's assessment of teachers is that the previous year's winner is asked to be a member of the following year's panel. This places them squarely within a paradigm shift that eludes most teachers over their careers. The national winners typically highlight collaborative efforts as essential to their approaches.

Part III provides detailed examinations of the collaborative efforts that GVSU's Gordon Andrews and WMU's Wilson Warren and James Cousins initiated with area high school history teachers and students, specifically those at PCHS and two Kalamazoo-area alternative high schools, Barclay Hills Educational Center and the Climax-Scotts Adult Alternative Education Program. More specifically, this section of the book explains the GVSU and WMU history educators' focus on historiography as a historical pedagogy to enhance and enrich students' learning of and interest in history.[13] The historiography project portion of the collaborative effort began during the 2011–2012 school year and continues to date.

Chapter 7 provides a baseline for understanding historiography's pedagogical potential by reviewing the relevant literature on how it has been or more often, has been suggested to be used with high school history students. This chapter not only surveys the literature on how historiography can be used at the high school level, but it especially highlights literature that suggests how collaborative models can be used in this process. This literature is often referenced in subsequent chapters as a touchstone for how this particular collaborative project varied from other models.

Chapter 8 examines the collaboration among GVSU and WMU history educators and PCHS history teachers. In particular, the chapter highlights the PCHS history teachers' reflections on the historiography project. Kent Baker, Sara Brown, Patricia Johnson, and Tama Salisbury have been the core teacher participants in the project since its origins. Baker is the school's

"History of the Americas" International Baccalaureate (IB) instructor. Johnson and Salisbury are the "Twentieth-Century World" IB instructors. Brown is the school's media center teacher-librarian. In 2014–2015, Sue Hoffman, one of the school's ninth-grade United States history (non-IB) instructors, also became part of the historiography project. One of the essential questions informing the collaboration's investigations was whether or not teachers would find the use of historiography in the classroom a useful method of instruction. Amid their myriad other responsibilities, this chapter addresses the varied ways teachers introduced historiography in the classroom over a three-year period, and whether, in fact, they found it useful. Equally significant to the successful use of historiography in the classroom was the collaboration of the media center's librarian and her staff. At a time when books and libraries are largely seen as superfluous, too expensive, or both (e.g., there are no libraries in 700 of New York City's 1,800 public schools and 160 of Chicago's 700 public schools), this book points to the necessity of the library.[14] To develop historically relevant research experiences, teachers, the high school librarian, and historians collaborated on the kinds of experiences students need to be successful in college and as citizens.

Chapter 9 looks at the historiography project's impacts on PCHS students, primarily those in the two IB classes, but also provides some preliminary observations about the impact of historiography on ninth-grade students' understanding of U.S. history. A guiding assumption of the project was that helping students to comprehend and appreciate the place of historiography would pique their curiosity and also provide them with deeper insights into the discipline itself. Additionally, the project hypothesized that in terms of citizenship education, students should understand that there are vibrant debates within the history profession. The historiography project therefore intentionally introduced opportunities to dispel the notion that history is "one damn thing after another." Because school is one of "the last shared democratic experiences that we have as a nation," it is imperative that our students be presented with extant and sometimes nuanced debates over what history means. Based on data collected in three years of the WMU, GVSU, and PCHS collaboration, this chapter will reveal the way historiography helps to remove the occlusions that so often prevent students from achieving a deeper level of historical understanding.[15]

From the beginning of the historiography project, it included a central role for pre-service teachers. Chapter 10 focuses on this part of the project's design and implementation. GVSU and WMU history educators' social studies methods students have led the panel discussions that formed a central part of the historiographical lessons. A natural outgrowth of the use of historiography in secondary classrooms is an examination of its place in the pre-service teacher training of history and social studies students.[16] The historiography project's design addresses this issue by including pre-service methods students from WMU and GVSU who participated in the reading of historiographies on a variety of U.S. and world history themes.

6 Introduction

This chapter explains the students' preparation to teach historiographical lessons and participate in panel discussions with the two IB classes from 2011 to date. Typically, these opportunities constituted the first time that most of the pre-service methods students had any substantive dealings with historiography; most were only vaguely familiar with the term before they started their teaching preparations.

Arguably one of the most significant areas of the historiography project's inquiry has been in terms of attempting to improve alternative education students' historical thinking skills. To say that there is a paucity of research involving historical thinking and alternative education is an understatement. Chapter 11 addresses that serious need. Beginning in 2013, WMU's James Cousins worked with history teachers and students at the Barclay Hills Educational Center and the Climax-Scotts Adult Alternative Education Program to investigate the use of historiography as a pedagogical tool for teaching history to alternative education students. Both schools' demographics reveal populations that are economically disadvantaged—almost all students are eligible for free and reduced meals—and racially isolated. Alternative education too frequently adopts the worst examples of educational Taylorism, subjecting students to the lowest form of online learning. Students are asked to complete courses online in Skinnerian fashion, watch online lectures, read, and then take a chapter quiz. This chapter investigates the historiography project's guiding hypothesis that all students can develop historical thinking skills.

This book offers the hope that educational Taylorism can be overturned if more collaboration occurs among concerned and committed educators. For any profound change to occur, there must be a paradigmatic shift away from the current adherence to the neo-liberal global educational reform movement model of educational reform toward a model of collaboration that honors the teaching of history as a craft. This book offers working models and reasonable suggestions that can be replicated with little or no fiduciary obligation. It does so by demonstrating how to connect the vital interests of already existing institutions, teachers, and administrators within our universities and K–12 schools. Indeed, the chapters in this book illustrate how these groups are already intertwined as vested groups in a dynamic mission. *Collaboration and the Future of Education* offers a model and suggestions for how these groups can find and learn from each other.

NOTES

1. Raymond E. Callahan, *Education and the Cult of Efficiency: A Study of the Social Forces That Have Shaped the Administration of the Public Schools* (Chicago: University of Chicago Press, 1962), 232–40.
2. Jonathan Rees, "Frederick Taylor in the Classroom: Standardized Testing and Scientific Management," *Radical Pedagogy* 3:2(2001). http://radicalpedagogy. icap.org/content/issue3.2 (accessed January 15, 2013).

Introduction 7

3. Ibid.

4. Descriptions of the various high school-level *TCI Alive!* textbooks can be found at: http://www.teachtci.com/programs/high-school-social-studies-textbooks-and-curriculum.html (accessed January 15, 2013).

5. Zalman Usiskin, "Do We Need National Standards with Teeth," *Educational Leadership* 65:3(2007), 42. Usiskin states, "National standards with teeth have a tacit assumption: Our teachers cannot be trusted to make decisions about which curriculum is best for their schools." This assumption lies at the heart of many administrators as they remove teacher decisions regarding curriculum, turning those duties over to publishers like *History Alive!*

6. Whereas these curricula appear new, they in fact subscribe to a well-documented array of traditional history approaches where teachers "cover" eras using texts and then require students to recall details on standardized tests with the same sorts of nonhistorical understanding. On these traditional approaches and their problems, see, for example, Larry Cuban, "History of Teaching in Social Studies," in *Handbook of Research on Social Studies Teaching and Learning*, ed. James P. Shaver (New York: Macmillan, 1991), 197–209; Linda S. Levstik, "NCSS and the Teaching of History," in *NCSS in Retrospect*, Bulletin 92, ed. O.L. Davis (Washington, DC: National Council for the Social Studies, 1996), 21–34; Peter Seixas, "Beyond 'Content' & 'Pedagogy': In Search of a Way to Talk about History Education," *Journal of Curriculum Studies* 31(1999), 317–31; and Bruce A. VanSledright, *The Challenge of Rethinking History Education: On Practices, Theories, and Policy* (New York: Routledge, 2011).

7. Katie Ash, "Curricula All Over the Map for Blended Classes," *Education Week* 30:15(January 12, 2011), S5–S7; and Grand Rapids Public Schools' *My Choice: 2012–2013 High School Curriculum Guide*, 14. A description of the blended curriculum can be found at: http:// grps.org/images/departments/academics/pdfs/curriculum_guide_2012–13.pdf (accessed January 15, 2013). See also Tony Tagliavia, "New Blended Curriculum in GRPS Combines Classroom Work, Computer Use Outside Room," WOOD TV 8, updated Tuesday, September 7, 2010. http://woodtv.com/dpp/news/education/back_to_school/new-blended-curriculum-for-GRPS-high-schools (accessed January 15, 2013).

8. Monica Scott, "Godfrey-Lee Schools Awarded $179,000 from State for Data Coach to Assess, Track Achievement," April 6, 2012. http://mlive.com/news/grand-rapids/index.ssf/2012/04/godfrey-lee_schools_gets_17900.html (accessed January 15, 2013).

9. For a recent balanced assessment of the pros and cons of "flipped" classrooms, see Ian Bogost, "The Condensed Classroom," *The Atlantic*, August 27, 2013 http://www.theatlantic.com/technology/archive/2013/08/the-condensed-classroom/279013/ (accessed December 15, 2015). Also see Judy E. Gaughan, "The Flipped Classroom in World History," *The History Teacher* 47:2(2014), 221–44. Gaughan's analysis of her flipped classroom's virtues are largely positive but may be due largely to the fact that at the college level she had complete control over the course design process.

10. These reforms ignore calls from the standards movement for deeper levels of historical thinking as outlined by the National Center for History in the Schools. http://www.nchs.ucla.edu/Standards/historical-thinking or the Common Core Standards for English and Language Arts & Literacy in the History/Social Studies: www.corestandards.org/assets/CCSSI_ELA%20Standards.pdf (both accessed January 15, 2013).

11. Gordon Andrews, Wilson J. Warren, and Sarah Drake Brown, "Crossing the Educational Rubicon without the TAH: Collaboration among University and Secondary-Level History Educators," *The History Teacher* 46:2(2013), 253–66.

8   *Introduction*

12. Grounding collaboration in local relationships is crucial. As Linda Symcox makes clear in "Forging New Partnerships: Collaboration between University Professors and Classroom Teachers to Improve History Teaching, 1983–2011," *The History Teacher* 45:3(2012), 359–82, the persistent cultural divide between the educational establishment and professional historians is largely due to the distance between the two groups. Partnerships and collaboration based on ongoing locally based projects can bridge this distance. Also see Victoria B. Fantozzi, "Divergent Purposes: A Case Study of a History Education Course Co-taught by a Historian and Social Studies Education Expert," *The History Teacher* 45:2(2012), 241–59.

13. See, for instance, Michael G. Lovorn, "Historiography in the Methods Course: Training Preservice History Teachers to Evaluate Local Historical Commemorations," *The History Teacher* 45:4(2012), 569–79; and Sam Wineburg, Daisy Martin, and Chauncey Monte-Sano, *Reading Like a Historian: Teaching Literacy in Middle and High School History Classrooms* (New York: Teachers College Press, 2011).

14. See Oliver Morrison, "Number of Libraries Dwindles in N.Y.C. Schools," *Education Week Online*, March 17, 2015. http://www.edweek.org/ew/articles/2015/03/18/number-of-libraries-dwindle-in-nyc-schools.html (accessed May 4, 2015); and Becky Vevea, "Losing School Librarians in Chicago Public Schools," *WBEZ91.5*, July 23, 2014. http:// www.wbez.org/news/losing-school-librarians-chicago-public-schools-110547 (accessed May 4, 2015).

15. Jonathan Kozol quoted in Jarrett Dapier, "Back to School in the Bronx," *In These Times* 36:11(2012), 34–35. http://inthesetimes.com/article/14027/back_to_school_in_the_bronx (accessed May 5, 2015).

16. Increased content knowledge and exposure to meaningful field experiences where content pedagogy is required of pre-service teachers has been called for in the American Council for Education's ACE Presidents' Task Force on Teacher Education, *To Touch the Future: Transforming the Way Teachers are Taught* (1999). The charge of the study was "to equip college and university presidents to lead the nation's campuses in a major improvement in the quality of education provided to teachers and school leaders." The call has gone largely unheeded.

Part I

The Current Landscape of History Education

Teaching history effectively requires teachers at all levels to have the freedom to immerse students in the authentic elements of the discipline. It also requires history teachers to have the abilities and dispositions necessary to support students' efforts. The current landscape of history education, however, and education in general at the K–12 levels especially, increasingly blocks or impedes teachers from pursuing this type of history instruction. Part I of the book explains some of the key impediments to high school history teachers' efforts to teach disciplinary skills. Partly due to the ways that educational Taylorism has eroded craft approaches to teaching, many history teachers have allowed textbook-driven instruction to erode their own voice and control over curriculum. Many high school history teachers are also focused almost exclusively on factually oriented lessons that do not allow them to teach historical thinking skills in their classrooms. Nevertheless, the landscape for history education is not entirely bleak. This portion of the book also describes projects—both national and local—that suggest that collaborative efforts can help to overcome the current impediments to more effective instruction. Providing this context is crucial in explaining how important collaboration among historians and history teachers is for the future of education. These perspectives are highlighted in Parts II and III.

2 *History Alive!* Is History Dead

Problems with Textbook-Driven Instruction

One of the last realms of relative autonomy for teachers is lesson content. State guidelines determine so-called scope and sequence of instruction. State standards, or content expectations, as Michigan describes them, determine the overall focus for each subject and grade level. Traditionally, specific curriculum decisions were left to individual school districts and teachers to map out. Yet in recent years even this level of the instructional process has been subject to increasing outside intervention and influence, especially through local school administrative and state government mandates.

A recent example of this outside influence on social studies in the state of Michigan is the Michigan Citizenship Collaborative Curriculum, or simply MC3. Developed between 2007 and 2013 by personnel from six school districts—Oakland Schools, Macomb Intermediate School District (ISD), Ottawa ISD, Ingham ISD, Genesee ISD, and Kent ISD—in collaboration with several other districts, MC3 is meant to provide curriculum materials that are rich yet uniform in terms of meeting the latest version of the state content expectations, which particularly for subjects like world history are quite ambitious and daunting. More recently, C3, or the College, Career, and Civic Life Framework for Social Studies State Standards, the result of collaboration among several national history and social studies organizations, which is meant to be used to help states implement the Common Core guidelines for literacy, is likely to significantly reshape state social studies curricula once again. As the framework highlights, the "C3 Framework is centered on an Inquiry Arc—a set of interlocking and mutually supportive ideas that frame the ways students learn social studies content."[1]

Another way in which outside entities have increasingly seized control of curricula from teachers and schools has been in terms of textbook choices. Textbook publishers, responding to the marketing opportunity provided by state standard revisions, now routinely provide content linked to the grade-level appropriate standards. In schools throughout southwest Michigan, TCI, or Teachers' Curriculum Institute, materials have been widely adopted. *History Alive!* is arguably the most popular U.S. history textbook among schools in the Kalamazoo area and perhaps statewide. Established in 1989, TCI's approach emphasizes virtually all the learning strategies and concerns

12   The Current Landscape of History Education

that were in vogue during the late twentieth century. The teachers' guide to middle and high school social studies starts by saying the TCI approach is based on three premises: 1. students have different learning styles; 2. cooperative interaction increases learning and improves social skills; 3. all students can learn. The teachers' guide goes on to elaborate further on eight features of the TCI approach: 1. theory-based active instruction; 2. standards-based content; 3. preview assignment; 4. multiple intelligences teaching strategies; 5. considerate text; 6. graphically organized reading notes; 7. processing assignments; and 8. multiple intelligence assessments. The TCI *Teaching Alive!* approach is ambitious and seems to address many of the student learning concerns that good teachers have. But does it embody authentic historical approaches and thinking skills?[2]

The history of history textbook use suggests that this is a daunting task. In 1937, one part of the American Historical Association's Report of the Commission on the Social Studies was *Methods of Instruction in the Social Studies*. A significant portion of the report on methods of instruction dealt with textbook use. Ernest Horn, author of the report, noted that the "textbook has been a dominant factor in the schools of the United States for more than a hundred years." Because of a longstanding dependence on textbooks, due to traditions of inadequately trained teachers, reform organizations, beginning with the AHA's Committee of Ten in 1892, reluctantly admitted that adoption and use of textbooks was essential. However, Horn noted several common problems with textbook dependence, including students' lack of reading ability, lack of visual and other graphic materials, and teachers' tendencies to rely exclusively on them for students' reading material. Horn also chided teachers for their use of textbooks in lieu of classroom discussion. He noted that too often teachers assumed that students would be able to read a textbook and be fully competent on its subject matter. His chief advice to teachers was to use collateral reading to gain new understandings. "One of the greatest contributions of collateral reading is the stimulation and development of present and continuing interests." He also advocated study of primary sources, contemporary literature, historical fiction, and other types of imaginative literature.[3]

Although Ernest Horn's *Methods of Instruction in the Social Studies* notes publishers' importance in determining textbooks' content, Frances Fitzgerald's *America Revisited*, published in 1979, was even more explicit in attributing American students' understandings of history to how their textbooks have presented the past. Fitzgerald asserts that "the system of adoptions has a significant impact on the way Americans are taught their own history." She elaborates on how private interest groups and citizens' organizations have influenced the way Americans have understood their past. She also points out that Americans' protests against textbook portrayals date back to the mid-nineteenth century. Perhaps her most telling point in regard to the influence of textbooks is that they make little difference in terms of specific student understandings of American history. Instead, they are best at creating impressions: "what sticks to the memory from those textbooks is not any particular series of facts but an atmosphere, an impression, a tone."[4]

Perhaps the most damning indictment of textbooks has been James W. Loewen's *Lies My Teacher Told Me: Everything Your American History Textbook Got Wrong*, published in 1995. Its highly accusatorial and inflammatory title not only piqued readers' concerns about textbook "lies," but it also helped to catapult the book to significant financial success. Loewen provides specific details about how multiple textbooks have distorted views of the European colonization of the Americas, treatment of the natives, slaves, and black Americans, and the federal government's actions, as well as propagating myths about America as a land of opportunity and ceaseless progress. Of course, by focusing on the notion of "lies," Loewen opens up the bigger question of what is historical "truth." Loewen seems to believe that historical truth is out there but that publishers have no interest in providing it.[5]

Whereas Loewen lavishes great attention on the way textbooks have skewed students' understanding of historical people, events, and issues, he does not ask publishers to focus more attention on the skills involved in constructing history. This topic is a major focus of David Kobrin's *Beyond the Textbook: Teaching History Using Documents and Primary Sources*, published in 1996. Like Fitzgerald and Loewen, Kobrin notes how publishers' concerns have impacted the way typical history textbooks are put together. He is also concerned how textbooks' "tone of authority" helps to squelch genuine interest among students in understanding how historical accounts are constructed. Indeed, the focus of his book is on how teachers and students can move beyond textbook narratives and begin to develop approaches, skills, and inclinations that would help them create their own historical insights and accounts.[6]

CAN HISTORY TEXTBOOKS DEVELOP HISTORICAL THINKING?

TCI's claim that it uses approaches that will help students better learn history is a bold one, especially given the lack of emphasis on skill-building in traditional history textbooks. Its focus on particular learning premises and features also do not square centrally with the array of skills associated with *historical thinking*. The scholarship associated with so-called historical thinking grew out of investigations into how young people understand the discipline's fundamental components. Here it is important to note that this use of the term historical thinking was certainly not the first such use. Paul Ward, for instance, wrote an interesting brief handbook for the American Historical Association in 1971, *Elements of Historical Thinking*, which was part of the AHA's Discussions on Teaching

14 The Current Landscape of History Education

Series, which built on an even earlier work published in 1959 called *A Style of History for Beginners*. Ward's handbook focused on three features of historical inquiry: "first, accenting and clarifying the separate pieces of evidence; second, seeing how well the assembled evidence tells the story and explains the whole situation; and third, highlighting the human dimension in the evidence." Ward's handbook focused on the key elements of how historians conduct research in a way that then might be translated to students.[7]

The modern scholarship associated with historical thinking was pioneered during the 1980s and 1990s—parallel to the period in which many of the approaches emphasized by TCI came into prominence. Scholars such as Peter Lee, Rosalyn Ashby, Peter Seixas, Keith Barton, Linda Levstik, Bruce VanSledright, and Sam Wineburg, all of whom adopted in varying degrees approaches pioneered by cognitive psychologists, studied how students grappled with the discipline's thorny concepts and implicit assumptions. The most famous book on historical thinking, Wineburg's *Historical Thinking and Other Unnatural Acts: Charting the Future of Teaching the Past*, explained research that highlighted how students read historical texts, contextualized historical documents, and conceptualized cultural assumptions. The scholarship that has developed since the book's publication has resonated with K–12 teachers and academics. Arguably, this has been true primarily because this research suggests that teaching and learning history is not only much more complicated than many assumed, but that it requires an understanding of historical processes that go well beyond the standard emphases of classroom teachers and college professors. Historical thinking research suggests that teachers' classroom instruction needs to make explicit elements of the discipline that are often assumed or left implicit. That is, history teachers' pedagogies need to better reflect the key components of the discipline and provide students with opportunities to practice such components.[8]

In an essay in the June 2011 issue of *Historically Speaking*, historian and history educator Fritz Fischer summarized some of the underlying assumptions of historical thinking scholarship. He noted nine major elements:

1. History is about questions, not answers.
2. Historians center their questions and inquiries on sources.
3. Historians use primary sources to understand the past and secondary sources to help contextualize the subject.
4. Historians look at and care about dates and chronology and study change and continuity over time.
5. Historians explore cause and effect. History is not merely "one damn thing after another."
6. Historians look at authorship.
7. Historians examine different points of view and multiple perspectives about events in the past.

8. Historians look at different kinds of sources and examine the intent and motivation behind each source.
9. Historians bring these sources together and make judgments and craft arguments about the past.

In a nutshell, historical thinking research suggests that the pedagogies that elementary and secondary teachers use replicate as much as possible the actual historical research methodologies that historians use.[9]

THE TCI APPROACH AND HISTORICAL THINKING

So how does the innovative and complex array of theories and pedagogical advice utilized in *History Alive!* line up with what historical thinking scholarship advocates? One way to examine this question is by comparing the key components of the TCI approach to the main elements of historical thinking research. The three major premises of the TCI approach—the belief that students have different learning styles, that they would benefit from cooperative learning in a way that improves social skills, and that all of them can learn—are not in conflict with any of the key elements of historical thinking. Nothing would prevent students from pursuing authentic historical investigation if they did so using different learning styles or in a cooperative fashion. Historians do not often work cooperatively, as is generally the case in the hard sciences, but that preference does not mean that students should not pursue historical research in a cooperative fashion. Given the proper training, inclinations, and opportunities, anyone can pursue historical research. Doing history is not like doing nuclear physics—special technical training and/or expensive lab equipment is not necessary.

Nevertheless, the eight features of the TCI approach are more problematic in terms of developing genuine historical thinking. The eight features of the TCI approach are: theory-based active instruction, specifically Howard Gardner's multiple intelligences, Elizabeth Cohen's cooperation interaction, and Jerome Bruner's spiral curriculum; standards-based content; preview assignment, akin to an anticipatory set; multiple intelligence teaching strategies; considerate text, or reading that is accessible to students' abilities; graphically organized reading notes; processing assignment or end-of-lesson assignments that challenge students to apply what they have learned; and multiple intelligence assessments. Whereas TCI claims that both its theoretical and pedagogical emphasize stress discovery, which is indeed central to historical thinking, this is not clear in terms of much of the TCI repertoire. For instance, multiple intelligences theory has more to say in terms of how young people express what they know; it does not really lend itself to helping students analyze historical documents, which tend to be mostly written materials. However, a creative teacher could supply students with an array of documents in which, for instance, a student with significant

16 *The Current Landscape of History Education*

musical-rhythmic intelligence might examine music from a particular place and time. However, much of what seems to be suggested in TCI materials focuses on allowing students to express historical ideas in their dominant intelligence. For instance, a student would express his or her historical ideas through song or dance (i.e., either the musical-rhythmic or body-kinesthetic intelligence). But of course, that begs the question of how they gathered their historical ideas in the first place, which, for historians, is the most important element of the discovery process.[10]

The TCI theoretical application that is probably closest to historical thinking is Jerome Bruner's spiral curriculum. Using this approach, curriculum materials start with exploration of an event, idea, or personality through observation, description, and identification and then "spiral" up to higher levels of cognitive thinking, such as application, analysis, synthesis, and evaluation. Historical investigation is based on a very similar process in which the historian starts by gathering and sifting through relevant evidence. After the historian considers how other historians have treated the same or similar issues, a process of higher-level thinking is applied to develop a meaningful interpretation of the primary and secondary source materials.[11]

As part of its advocacy of multiple intelligence teaching strategies, TCI's pedagogical advice includes use of visual source material. Although some prominent history educators like Sam Wineburg have been less than enthusiastic about having students focus on visual source materials, such materials have been the focus of many historians' research.[12] In addition to their use as primary materials, significant work has been done on how to incorporate historical film as a secondary source into students' research. Yet this sort of focus is not part of the TCI approach. Instead the TCI pedagogical suggestions seem distinctly *ahistorical*: 1. use powerful images to teach social studies concepts (comment: what *is* a powerful image?); 2. arrange your classroom so projected images will be large and clear (comment: isn't this common sense?); 3. ask carefully sequenced questions that lead to discovery (comment: again, isn't this common sense?); 4. challenge students to read about the image and apply what they learn (comment: so, where's the visual history focus?); and 5. have students interact with the images to demonstrate what they have learned (comment: this focus seems to illustrate how the TCI multiple intelligences focus has more to do with how students show what they know than it does with actual source exploration).

Included in TCI's additional advice about multiple intelligence teaching strategies, teachers are urged to have students "write for understanding." Any historical thinking advocate would stress that writing is not an "add on." Writing is an essential part of the historical process. Indeed, there is no historical understanding *without* writing. But the TCI approach to writing seems vacuous: 1. use writing to help your students learn key social studies concepts (comment: this makes it seem as although the focus is the concepts and not the use of concepts to convey higher-level thinking); 2. give students rich experiences to write about (comment: this is fine except that no suggestion about having students use real historical sources is included); 3. have students record their ideas, thoughts, and feelings in prewriting activities (comment: again, this is fine, but no specific advice about how they should do so is offered—a strategy for note-taking, for example, would be immensely helpful if students are to actually do historical research); 4. provide students with authentic writing assignments (comment: this is great except nearly all the examples cited are ones in which students create their *own* sources instead of writing about actual sources); and 5. guide students through the writing process (comment: this begs several questions: What writing process? What's the focus of the writing? Shouldn't a heuristic for the students' efforts be provided?).

The focus of the fifth of the eight TCI approaches is what is termed "considerate text." The teachers' manual points out the unfortunate fact that students need to learn how to read a textbook. This is indeed a tragic fact of the American K–12 educational system; textbooks are ubiquitous at all levels of the formal educational process, including college. TCI goes on to plug its clear, well-organized, comprehensible, manageable textbooks that use clear and helpful images and graphic organizers. Teachers are given additional advice about strategies for helping students read their TCI textbook, including prereading strategies, anticipation guides, KWL strategies, and guiding questions. If the end goal of an educational process is mastery of textbook material, then the means suggested would be exemplary. However, reading skills for the real world, and certainly in the realm of historical investigation, require abilities that go well beyond reading something that is "easy to read." The real world of historical written materials includes all sorts of items that put a premium on contextualization, interpretation and interpolation, and even intuitive guesswork. It would be nice if a student was only going to encounter items after high school that were like TCI textbooks, but that just isn't the case. Indeed, the new Common Core Standards for Language Arts point out the need for secondary school students to analyze and evaluate complex literature. Students are urged to integrate wide-ranging literary materials. Again, effective reading requires tackling *inconsiderate* as much as considerate text.

The teachers' guides for the TCI United States History Program of *History Alive!* are even more revealing in terms of demonstrating a disconnect between this curriculum and genuine historical thinking activities.[13] For each of the sections that correlate to a chapter in the text, the guides focus on a specific activity drawing upon the eight features of the TCI approach. In the guide for the 1890–1920 period, Activity 2.1 is titled "Experiencing the Assembly Line." According to the guide, the activity "is designed to have students experience the monotony and repetition of work on the assembly line. By assuming the role of assembly line workers to repetitiously recreate one part of a drawing of a man, students will be better able to understand how the specialization of labor and the move to assembly line production

18   *The Current Landscape of History Education*

impacted workers around the turn of the century." The activity instructions go on to describe how students will produce detailed pictures of a man that will then be translated into production of "high-quality paper dolls." Students are then asked to produce as many drawings of a man as they can in a twenty-minute period. A factory manager and quality control supervisor are then appointed to yell at students to work harder and keep up the pace.

On the surface, this sounds like a useful experiential exercise. But if one knows anything about the history of assembly line production during the second industrial revolution, the activity skews what actually happened. The most important innovation of this era of industrialization was not the speed-up but Taylorization (or scientific management). That is, the focus of worker-management clashes was primarily over loss of control over the production process (deskilling) followed by introduction of incentive pay (or piece-work) systems. A more authentic exercise along the same lines would start with students being told to hand over their complete drawings of a man to a manager who would then choose the most elaborate one and tell each student to produce one part of the drawing over and over. Students should then be presented with target quotas for the twenty-minute period that are based on the greatest number of pieces of the drawing that the most productive student had produced. Some students might reach the quota and receive a bonus. But the quota would be high enough that many would not. After discussion of the pros and cons of this system, students should be asked to read selections from Frederick Winslow Taylor's *The Principles of Scientific Management* (1911). Taylor's prose is straightforward and understandable for young people, so a few pages could be read and discussed with an eye to understanding why Taylor wanted to make these changes.

Another lesson suggestion in the teachers' guide that is similarly lacking in terms of authentic historical context and direction is in the "Roaring Twenties and Great Depression" collection. Activity 4.1 is titled "My Deal: What Should Be Done About the Great Depression." The focus of the activity is a collaborative exercise in which small groups of students are asked to role play economists who discuss four major economic problems of the Depression: overproduction, unequal distribution of wealth, high unemployment, and poverty. Students read concise briefings on each of the four economic problems and then deliberate on the most effective response using critical thinking questions that are divided into conservative, liberal, and radical options. The students are also supposed to consider part of the historical context for this important issue by reading about Herbert Hoover's conservative approach to the Depression and how that approach failed miserably.

There are major problems with the way this exercise is outlined. The most important is the notion that the responses that President Roosevelt considered could be pigeon-holed into these three distinct categories. Roosevelt was a pragmatist *par excellence*. His cabinet included a range of economists with widely varying ideologies and even mixes of ideologies. FDR himself started as a fiscal conservative who then became a supporter of Keynesian fiscal policy. Indeed, one of the most telling indications of the divided nature of FDR's administrations on economic issues was the debate about the causes of the 1936–1938 economic recession and the battle that ensued among his advisors over how to respond. Perhaps a more effective role play activity would be to take this particular historical incident, have students read an overview of it, perhaps using the excellent brief summary found in Patrick Renshaw's 1999 *Journal of Contemporary History* article on the topic, and then have students role play how FDR made his decision to side with the advisors who advocated Keynesian pump-priming.[14] He made this decision after hearing many different economic perspectives. Setting up the exercise this way would better convey the underlying pragmatism that so characterized how the New Deal and FDR functioned.

To be fair, one can find some useful activities suggested in the *History Alive!* teachers' guide. For instance, in the "Roaring Twenties and the Great Depression" guide, Activity 3.2: "Empathizing with the Victims of the Great Depression," focuses on Dorothea Lange's photographs and field notes. In this lesson, students take on the personae of a photographer for the Farm Security Agency, one of the notable New Deal programs. They are introduced to the work of Dorothea Lange's efforts in this role as a guide. After learning about her, students are then given examples of her field notes and asked to examine actual New Deal photos portraying the conditions of agricultural workers. Although students are asked to write their own field notes using imaginary details to embellish the data, the process they use seems pretty closely in line with how a historian would operate in a similar situation. The assignment culminates in the students writing a letter to President Roosevelt, based on their notes, describing the hardships faced by farmers whose lives had been ravaged by the Depression.

NO SUBSTITUTE FOR TEACHERS' DISCIPLINARY UNDERSTANDING

Although TCI's *History Alive!* embodies creative learning strategies, much of what it provides teachers would not help them develop students' historical thinking skills. The major problem with *History Alive!* is that it is not grounded in an understanding of what historians actually do. Perhaps the biggest disconnect between *History Alive!* and historical thinking is in terms of Fritz Fischer's second point about historical thinking: *historians center their questions and inquiries on sources.* Indeed, there seems to be very little actual student exposure to source material in the *History Alive!* teachers' materials and the supporting pedagogical advice. A disproportionate amount of attention is directed to creative ways for students to demonstrate their ideas, but if their findings are not based on real historical materials then it is hard to see where the actual history is.

20 The Current Landscape of History Education

A better approach to the development of students' skills in analyzing historical sources, which would not necessarily preclude teachers from using ideas from texts such as *History Alive!*, would be to use one of the plethora of online sites that offer access to digitized primary sources in American history, such as American Memory from the Library of Congress. Once a teacher selects relevant documents, he or she could then have students closely read and analyze a source or related sources on a topic using the scaffolding guidance provided by one of the many heuristics provided by a multitude of sources. For instance, the Library of Congress's website offers a "Primary Source Analysis Tool" that can help students with this task. Another very useful analytical heuristic is the SCIM-C strategy that David Hicks, Peter E. Doolittle, and E. Thomas Ewing have developed. This particular heuristic provides students with a systematic method that asks them to closely examine a primary source by summarizing, contextualizing, inferring, monitoring, and then corroborating their insights. A teacher who asks students to investigate historical materials using this type of intensive analytical heuristic needs to provide support for their efforts from a position of informed understanding of the content area. That is, teachers need to know enough history to provide guidance for students to gain deeper understanding.[15]

Ultimately, there is no substitute for teachers' understanding of their content area. Even if *History Alive!* included many more examples of authentic historical thinking activities, a teacher who did not understand much about the discipline would be hard pressed to know how to effectively teach this to students. There is no magic bullet when it comes to teaching history. If one accepts this as true, then there really is no substitute for teacher control over the content that they teach. Only by grappling with real historical materials and trying to decipher their meanings can teachers develop their craft in a way that can help students in a meaningful way.

NOTES

1. On MC3, see http://oaklandk-12public.rubiconatlas.org/Atlas/Browse/View/Calendars (accessed July 15, 2013) and, on C3, see National Council for the Social Studies (NCSS), *The College, Career, and Civic Life (C3) Framework for Social Studies State Standards: Guidance for Enhancing the Rigor of K–12 Civics, Economics, Geography, and History* (Silver Spring, MD: NCSS, 2013).
2. *Bring Learning Alive!: The TCI Approach for Middle and High School Social Studies*, Rev. Ed. (Palo Alto, CA: Teachers' Curriculum Institute, 2005). Part I of the book elaborates on this approach.
3. Ernest Horn, *Methods of Instruction in the Social Studies*, Report of the Commission on the Social Studies, Part XV (New York: Charles Scribner's Sons, 1937), 206–99. Quoted on pp. 207 and 231.
4. Frances Fitzgerald, *America Revised: History Schoolbooks in the Twentieth Century* (Boston: Little, Brown and Company, 1979), 7–47. Quoted on pp. 18 and 34.

History Alive! *Is History Dead* 21

5. James W. Loewen, *Lies My Teacher Told Me: Everything Your American History Textbook Got Wrong* (New York: The New Press, 1995).
6. David Kobrin, *Beyond the Textbook: Teaching History Using Documents and Primary Sources* (Portsmouth, NH: Heinemann, 1996), 3–5. Quoted on p. 4.
7. Paul L. Ward, *Elements of Historical Thinking* (Washington, DC: American Historical Association, 1971).Quoted on pp. 4–5.
8. Illustrative examples of these scholars' pioneering investigatory work on historical thinking include: Peter Lee and Rosalyn Ashby, "Progression in Historical Understanding among Students Ages 7–14," in *Knowing, Teaching, and Learning History: National and International Perspectives*, ed. Peter N. Stearns, Peter Seixas, and Sam Wineburg (New York: New York University Press, 2000), 199–222; Peter Seixas, "Confronting the Moral Frames of Popular Film: Young People Respond to Historical Revisionism," *American Journal of Education* 102:3(1994), 261–85; Keith Barton and Linda S. Levstik, "'It Wasn't a Good Part of History': National Identity and Students' Explanations of Historical Significance," *Teachers College Record* 99:3(1998), 478–513; Levstik, "Articulating the Silences: Teachers' and Adolescents' Conceptions of Historical Significance," in *Knowing, Teaching, and Learning History*, 284–305; Bruce VanSledright, *In Search of America's Past: Learning to Read History in Elementary School* (New York: Teachers College Press, 2002); and Sam Wineburg, *Historical Thinking and Other Unnatural Acts: Charting the Future of Teaching the Past* (Philadelphia: Temple University Press, 2001).
9. Fritz Fischer, "The Historian as Translator: Historical Thinking, the Rosetta Stone of History Education," *Historically Speaking* 12:3(2011), 15–17. Also see Fischer, *The Memory Hole: The U.S. History Curriculum Under Siege* (Charlotte, NC: Information Age Publishing, 2014).
10. *Bring Learning Alive!*, 9–133. On the incorporation of multiple intelligences theory into educational practice, see Jack Schneider, *From the Ivory Tower to the Schoolhouse: How Scholarship Becomes Common Knowledge in Education* (Cambridge, MA: Harvard Education Press, 2014), 51–77. Schneider emphasizes how Howard Gardner was often leery of how textbook publishers and educators adapted his multiple intelligences theory for their uses.
11. *Bring Learning Alive!*, 16–17; and Jerome Bruner, *The Process of Education* (Cambridge, MA: Harvard University Press, 1960).
12. See, for example, Sam Wineburg and Daisy Martin, "Reading and Rewriting History," *Educational Leadership* 62:1(2004), 42–45.
13. History Alive! Teachers' Curriculum Institute, United States History Program. *The United States Coming of Age: 1890–1920* (Palo Alto, CA: Teachers' Curriculum Institute, 1999); and History Alive! Teachers' Curriculum Institute, United States History Program. *The Roaring Twenties and the Great Depression* (Palo Alto, CA: Teachers' Curriculum Institute, 1999).
14. Patrick Renshaw, "Was There a Keynesian Economy in the USA between 1933 and 1945," *Journal of Contemporary History* 34:3(1999), 337–64.
15. David Hicks, Peter E. Doolittle, and E. Thomas Ewing, "The SCIM-C Strategy: Expert Historians, Historical Inquiry, and Multimedia," *Social Education* 68:3(2004), 221–25.

3 The Teaching American History Project
Teachers' Assessments of Its Classroom Connection

Brainchild of the late Senator Robert C. Byrd, Democrat from West Virginia, the TAH Project was introduced as part of the 2001 education appropriation budget. Intended to improve the teaching of U.S. history—divorced from any connection to social studies—the project required applicants to submit proposals that would create partnerships among university educators, historians involved in museums or other public history agencies, and local education agencies, primarily public school districts or larger regional consortiums of public schools. Most projects were funded for three years in the range of $500,000 to $1 million. The purpose of these partnerships was the creation of opportunities for elementary, middle, and high school teachers to engage in intensive and authentic historical study. Byrd's concern and assumption was that teachers lacked sufficient content knowledge. Indeed, a National Center for Education Statistics report in 1997 indicated that over 80 percent of middle and high school teachers had neither majored nor minored in history. After Congress approved the legislation, requests for proposals for the new project appeared in the Federal Register in May 2001. Applicants then rushed to submit proposals for a July deadline, and the first grant recipients were selected in September of that year. Early in the project's history, proposals had to address Byrd's interest in the improvement of "traditional" United States history, typically political or constitutional history. However, over the years this requirement became increasingly marginal in the evaluation process. In the dozen years of the project's existence, well over $1 billion was allocated for hundreds of projects located in every state.[1]

Although the jury is still out on the long-term effectiveness of the project in improving teachers' historical knowledge, there is no doubt that thousands of teachers' historical interests were piqued at least for some time. Aside from its relatively brief period of emphasis on "traditional" history, the TAH encouraged teachers and academics to collaborate on project designs that were not linked to textbooks or technology-based curricula. Many of the projects pursued innovative emphases on historical methodologies, source analyses, and production of historical materials for classroom use. To date, however, scholarly assessments of the TAH's effectiveness and impact are difficult to generalize about since there were so many grants awarded in dozens of locations in all fifty states, each of which involved a wide range of emphases. The varied nature and impact of the TAH is evident in Rachel G. Ragland and Kelly A. Woestman's edited collection, *The Teaching American History Project: Lessons for History Educators and Historians*, published in 2009. One of the overarching themes evident in the essays is the importance of collaboration that stems from truly joint efforts by K–12 teachers and professional historians. Another is that professional historians collaborated best when they were open to K–12 teachers' perspectives and concerns. The collection also stresses the importance of content-based professional development. However, since the collection was published before the project came to an end, it does not attempt to provide an overall assessment of its impact.[2]

While still limited, the scholarly literature is increasing on the TAH's value and impact. Emphasizing ways that teachers might better think and teach historically, Kevin B. Sheets explains an exciting collaborative TAH project centered on having teachers use a variety of primary and secondary sources to create lesson plans framed around questions on early American history through an examination of Seneca Falls, New York. Sheets outlines how teachers might discover, as opposed to memorize, the past in ways that give them practice in using historically authentic skills and sources. He stresses how teachers need purposeful professional development that results in projects they can use in their classrooms.[3]

Kelly Ann Long's focus on TAH partnerships emphasizes the importance of creating and maintaining sustained collaboration. She explains in depth the importance of historians providing the resource base for teachers to create inquiry-based lessons as crucial to the development of sustained collaboration. When the focus is on high-quality, higher-order teaching and lessons, she posits that historians will learn from the classroom teachers and vice versa. In this way, real collaboration is a process of reciprocal learning. Yet arguably her most telling point is that genuine collaboration among educators in the schools and the academy would require the professoriate to revise its views of the tenure and reward systems that are longstanding in higher education. That is, tenure and promotion systems would need to reward professors who collaborate with K–12 teachers.[4]

The U.S. Department of Education's final report on the Teaching American History project emphasized that teachers universally valued the exposure to high-quality content-based professional development. It also noted that the networks established through the project would likely continue in many cases. Based primarily on a study of sixteen TAH projects in 2006, the report noted that these projects effectively used professional development practices that combined history content and pedagogy, particularly in terms of demonstrating approaches to effective use of primary source materials. The report also noted, however, that recruitment of teachers in need of help in these areas was uneven, that projects rarely involved

24   *The Current Landscape of History Education*

teachers from entire school districts, and that there was little evidence to show that the project had impacted student achievement. Indeed, the report pointed out that the various projects' focus on skills was generally not in alignment with state history assessments' emphases on information retention.[5]

The existing literature on TAH projects not only suggests ways in which collaboration among K–12 teachers and professional historians created new understandings, but it also points to ways in which both K–12 teachers and professional historians are deficient in terms of being able to help each other more effectively. The following summary of summer institute evaluation data from one such project illuminates areas in which all those involved in the historical teaching endeavor need to improve in order to better be able to collaborate.

KALAMAZOO REGIONAL EDUCATIONAL SERVICE AGENCY'S SUMMER INSTITUTES FOR TEACHING AMERICAN HISTORY

From 2004 to 2012, the Kalamazoo Regional Educational Service Agency (KRESA) partnered with Western Michigan University's History Department and the Kalamazoo Valley Museum for four three-year TAH grant projects. KRESA is part of the state of Michigan's intermediate and regional network of public school agencies with various functions for supporting and providing educational services. The partnership's major focus was sponsorship of summer institutes for K–12 teachers. In 2006, 2008, and 2010, two TAH projects were underway under KRESA's aegis. Wilson Warren from WMU's History Department coordinated the instructional portions of each of the four projects. KRESA's project managers recruited teachers for the summer institutes and then scheduled and facilitated the various logistical elements involved in the instruction. Tom Dietz and Elspeth Inglis from the Kalamazoo Valley Museum also provided instruction and participated in planning and implementing the field trip portions of each of the grant projects.

Over the 2004 to 2012 period, one of the summer institutes (2004–2006) focused on issues that are part of Michigan's high school U.S. history curriculum, one summer institute (2006–2008) emphasized U.S. issues taught in the middle school (eighth grade) curriculum, one (2008–2010) highlighted issues taught in both the fifth- and eighth-grade curricula that attracted a mix of elementary and middle school teachers, and one (2010–2012) stressed issues taught in both the eighth grade and high school curricula. The latter two grants were intentionally designed to attract teachers from different levels of schools since elementary, middle, and high school teachers rarely have a chance to interact with each other in any consistent or content-related fashion.

The summer institutes' general design was fairly consistent among the four grants. For each grant, three instructors with different specialties in the time period covered in the workshops provided instruction. A total of eight professors, including Wilson Warren, from Western Michigan University's History Department served as instructors as well as two professors from the University of Illinois-Chicago's History Department, and one professor each from the History Departments at Grand Valley State University, Central Michigan University, and the College of the Holy Cross. Each summer institute also featured a public history component that was linked to a field trip to a site featuring material culture from the period. During the four grants, the teachers participated in study trips to the Gerald Ford Presidential Museum, Gilmore Car Museum, Henry Ford Museum, Greenfield Village, Pullman Historic District, Chicago Historical Museum, Fort Michilimackinac, and various local museums in the Kalamazoo area, including the Kalamazoo Valley Museum, which was part of each summer institute's experience. In each summer institute, teachers had the option of earning either state credit equivalency units—needed as proof of professional development participation—or graduate credit from Western Michigan University's History Department by completing either a research paper or a detailed lesson plan. Over the span of the four grants, different combinations of research papers or lesson plans were tried.

Typically, twenty to thirty teachers participated in each summer institute session. The teachers' background in formal history coursework and even more so, genuine historical methodology varied tremendously. The middle and high school teachers normally had the most preparation in American history coursework, though very few of them had any graduate preparation in history that would have enhanced their understanding of historical methodology. For instance, twenty-seven middle-school teachers were part of the 2006 summer institute on nineteenth-century America. Although the teachers' classroom experience ranged from one year to thirty-three years, the average teacher had thirteen years of experience. Fifteen of the twenty-seven teachers also had master's degrees, all of them were in some area of education. Nearly all of them noted the American Revolution or the Civil War as areas of special interest.

That same summer, twenty-five teachers participated in a high school summer institute on twentieth-century topics. Although not quite as populated by veteran teachers, the average number of years of experience was ten. Nine of the twenty-five teachers had master's degrees, including three in a social science or history. In 2010, twenty-six mostly veteran teachers participated in a summer institute on the Gilded Age and Progressive Era. The average number of years of classroom experience was sixteen, with only four of the teachers having less than five years of teaching under their belts. Ten of the twenty-six teachers had master's degrees, but only three of those ten were in history. The other seven were in various educational fields. In

26 The Current Landscape of History Education

terms of interests, nearly all the participants named topics such as populism, progressivism, the labor movement, industrialization, urbanization, and World War I. In general, the 2010 cohort, which was not dissimilar from the other institutes focused on either middle or high school U.S. history areas, included veteran teachers with fairly significant educational credentials and a wide range of interests.

While collaboration among the university and elementary and secondary school participants was a primary goal as well as mandate of the grant itself, the degree to which collaborative efforts unfolded among the participants in each summer institute session depended upon a shared sense of professional goals and desires. In practice, collaboration was often challenging to achieve. The professors who led the instruction had content and methodological concerns that often did not intersect with the concerns of the various groups of elementary and secondary teachers. Examining the teachers' evaluations and comments from the sessions not only illuminates this central quandary, but it also points to ways in which collaboration might better work to promote deeper historical understanding in terms of other shared historical endeavors.[6]

THE TEACHERS' EVALUATIONS

An examination of the elementary and secondary school participants' written evaluations of the summer institutes from June 2004 through June 2011 suggests that teachers had a fairly stable set of likes and dislikes about the sessions that varied relatively little across the array of different content emphases and different instructors. Regarding what they found most valuable, teachers' comments generally fell into one of five categories: receiving new ideas and information; seeing new artifacts; seeing new places; gaining new perspectives on historical issues; and learning about primary sources. Typically the teachers rated positively any introduction to topics with which they were previously unfamiliar. For instance, Professor Nora Faires's presentations for the 2004–2006 high school summer institutes included discussion about what the 1893 Chicago World's Fair revealed about American society and culture at the time. Teachers found her presentations on the topic to be novel and exciting. Kalamazoo Valley Museum curators Tom Dietz and Elspeth Inglis's presentations each summer incorporated artifacts from the museum's local history collection in their discussions. These presentations were always well received. Each summer institute included various field trips to sites of historical relevance and/or museums that focused on pertinent topics. Aside from occasional concerns about logistics or weather, teachers universally found the sites themselves to be of great interest. Many expressed concerns about their ability to actually take students to the sites since field trips have largely been abandoned by schools, but they nevertheless said they learned a lot from the visits and could introduce what they learned in their own classrooms. Although a bit more mixed in terms of commentary, as noted below, teachers typically appreciated exposure to new perspectives and interpretations. Praise for the interpretations provided in the session readings was usually minimal, while speakers' interpretations were more often cited as worthwhile. For instance, one teacher commended Professor Robert Johnston's sessions in June 2010 this way: "The opportunity to engage in a scholarly discussion with our peers and an intellectual of Robert's caliber is not an opportunity teacher get to [sic] often after we are done with our degrees." Finally, while secondary readings were seldom praised, readings that included primary materials were often singled out for commendation. Many teachers noted that exposure to new primary sources had given them ideas about how to use such materials with their own students.

Teachers' concerns were more diffuse and more difficult to categorize. Many concerns stemmed from the participants' views about the practical implications and applications of the summer institutes' content and approaches. For instance, each summer, teachers noted that they had expected to receive specific help with lesson planning. Interestingly, in several years of the summer institutes, production of a detailed lesson plan was an option for those teachers seeking graduate credit, but teachers typically did not see their efforts as particularly valuable; they apparently wanted their institute instructors to provide them with lesson plans. Of course, most of the instructors did not use lesson plans *per se* in their college classes and were generally mystified with the specificity that teachers expected with such teaching materials. This concern was often tied to a similar concern about the informational dimensions of the summer institutes. Teachers would often note in their comments that they had expected more "practical" (i.e., teachable) information rather than information meant to help the teachers develop a background understanding of the various historical issues.

Another category of elementary and secondary teachers' concerns would be familiar to any college instructor who has been evaluated by students. Teachers fairly regularly noted that there was too much lecture and not enough activity. Here again, college instructors, as they generally do in their own college teaching environments, saw themselves as primarily information and interpretation providers. This conception of the instructors' role occasionally ran up against the elementary and especially, secondary teachers' views of themselves as competent professionals. For instance, one participant in the 2006 high school summer institute said: "I wish the college professors would have spent more time preparing their lessons/presentations for those of us who teach at the high school level. I felt like I took college lectures/classes all over again." Another participant that same year noted: "Drop the day long lectures on topics we already learned about as undergraduates." Of course, in nearly every session, there were participants

28 The Current Landscape of History Education

who were grateful for the in-depth and information-dense presentations, but a notable minority of the secondary-level teachers typically expressed concerns that the emphasis on lecture was in some way demeaning of their standing as professionals.

For many of those concerned about a lecture emphasis, their preference seems to have been for more focus on innovative teaching techniques and activities. Some noted a desire for more emphasis on technology, especially in terms of visual materials. One of the most popular of the presenters, Professor Edward O'Donnell from Holy Cross College, received consistent praise for his use of visual information. One participant in the 2010 summer institute said: "Dr. O'Donnell did a great job with photos and helped us to see how useful they can be." Another that year said: "Dr. O'Donnell was very informative and introduced concepts in ways that helped me understand the period better. I really appreciated the discussion of images and the very real discussion of immigrant groups." Interestingly, while Professor O'Donnell lectured with the use of visuals almost exclusively, he was not typically criticized for excessive talking. It seems that his use of visual materials augmented his lecture focus enough to satisfy teachers' concerns about excessive talking.

Several instructors used a variety of primary source analysis activities about which teachers expressed mixed opinions. While modeling such activities was in fact one of the ways that everyone involved in the summer institutes hoped we could provide teachers with authentic examples of classroom activities, many teachers did not make this connection. Some expressed misgivings about how applicable such emphases would be with their own students, especially in the case of the elementary and middle school teachers. For example, in the 2009 summer institute on early America for elementary school teachers, teachers noted, despite all three instructors' use of primary source activities, that they wanted "some 'kid' friendly materials to use with 4th grade kids," "more connections to elementary actual lessons," and "relevant examples of lessons to use in an upper elementary classroom." For the teachers who expressed praise and support for the primary source activities, many simply wanted more time built into the sessions for pursuing the activities in more depth.

A recurring comment by teachers was dismay that the summer institutes did not provide specific lesson materials and activities. Perhaps especially for the teachers familiar with much of the professional development available at the elementary and secondary school level, the summer institutes seemed to strike them as overly academic and focused on issues at a rarified level not associated with teaching young people. The instructors and all of the planners involved in designing the summer institutes tended to see their task as educating the educators. A fair number of the teachers wanted the sessions to be more directly focused on the process of teaching history in their classes rather than on the intellectual tools that might inform their own design of teaching activities.

The Teaching American History Project 29

LESSONS FOR COLLABORATION

Based on several years of teachers' written evaluations, teachers' comments during the institutes, and general observations about the summer institutes, three main lessons for collaboration seem clear. The first, and perhaps the most important, is that for collaboration to work among college professors of history and K–12 history teachers, it is essential that the college professors need to have a strong basic understanding of the confines and contours of how the K–12 world of history teaching works. Whereas most college professors see teaching as an opportunity to exercise their creativity and ingenuity to craft lessons about areas that illuminate the most important dimensions of how they view their fields, elementary and secondary teachers are more often bound, and arguably constrained, by how various levels of standards and curricula—national, state, and local—define their topics. It is essential that college professors have some basic familiarity with relevant standards and engage them in a way that helps illuminate how teachers can work with them effectively. Professors need to frame their theoretical discussions in ways that intersect with the confines of the standards that teachers are faced with. Professors need to read about the standards that affect the teachers that they work with, think about the implications of those standards on the historical perspectives and issues that they feel strongly about, and consider the ways in which their own historical perspectives can intersect effectively with the ways in which K–12 historical standards constrain or define a particular field.

A second lesson is that creating greater understanding among professors about the dimensions and dynamics of lesson planning is a more difficult task but is also crucial for real collaboration. Perhaps the best way to collaborate at this level is for professors to think about the more discrete and specific elements of their fields that can be explained in parts and that might lend themselves to elementary or secondary teachers' lesson plan designs and activities. A topic like the 1893 World's Columbian Exposition, or simply Chicago World's Fair, is useful to think about in this regard. As noted, when Professor Faires presented on this topic, virtually all the high school teachers found it quite interesting. However, many also thought it was too narrow or insignificant an event for them to spend much time on in their classes. Secondary school history teachers tend to think of their task as explaining major developments in a way that does not allow the students to actually delve into topics in an exploratory or analytical way. Thus, the role of a professor in helping to collaborate with high school teachers on a topic like the 1893 World's Fair is to explain the various elements of the fair's significance that can be examined in depth and in a way that does not simply interrupt the flow of their overall narrative approach. Elements of the fair's importance in terms of its introduction of new cultural trends, for instance in promoting new convenience foods such as Aunt Jemima Pancake Mix, Juicy Fruit gum, and Cracker Jack, can be explained in a way that then fit into the larger

30 The Current Landscape of History Education

explanatory narratives that are the staple of high school teaching. Here, too, professors might explain how to use primary source materials with students so they can investigate specific exhibits and then attempt to generalize about how the fair influenced or precipitated future developments.

Finally, a third area of importance in terms of collaboration is more thoughtful engagement about the uses of instructional technology. To a degree perhaps even more imperative than in higher education, elementary and secondary teachers are increasingly expected to use instructional technology as a means to engage their students. Almost any new or relatively new elementary or secondary school classroom in the United States is replete with wireless Internet, smart boards, projectors, and other technological aids that make many college and university classrooms seem downright antiquated. With the equipment and access comes an expectation that the expensive resources will be used. Given the explosion of materials available as well as research on the ways that students learn, it may be most logical for professors to focus on visual media and ways that elementary and secondary teachers might not only illustrate historical trends but actually develop their students' investigatory skills. As they should, history professors tend to focus most of their attention on reading texts of various sorts. But modeling the ways in which visual materials—such as images and film—can be critically analyzed is important as well. Elementary and secondary teachers often hope to use visual materials to engage students in ways that primary, secondary, and tertiary texts may not. Unlike those who worry that the visual media might trump the use of literary materials, the two should be used in tandem to reinforce similar types of analytical skills.

NOTES

1. On the origins of the TAH project, see Alex Stein, "The Teaching American History Program: An Introduction and Overview," *The History Teacher* 36:2(February 2003), 178–85.
2. Rachel G. Ragland and Kelly A. Woestman, eds., *The Teaching American History Project: Lessons for History Educators and Historians* (New York: Routledge, 2009). Also see Rachel G. Ragland, "Sustaining Changes in History Teachers' Core Instructional Practices: Impact of *Teaching American History* Ten Years Later," *The History Teacher* 48:4(2015), 609–40.
3. Kevin B. Sheets, "Thinking Historically, Teaching Historically: Perspectives on the Professional Development of Teachers from a Teaching American History Grant," *The History Teacher* 43:3(May 2010), 455–61.
4. Kelly Ann Long, "Reflections on TAH and the Historian's Role: Reciprocal Exchanges and Transformative Contributions to History Education," *The History Teacher* 39:4(August 2006), 493–508.
5. U.S. Department of Education, Office of Planning, Evaluation and Policy Development, Policy and Program Studies Service, *Teaching American History Evaluation: Final Report* (Menlo Park, CA: SRI International, 2011).
6. On the TAH's attempt to bridge the various divides among history professors and K–12 history teachers, see, for instance, Kelly A. Woestman, "Teachers as Historians: A Historian's Experiences with TAH Projects," in *The Teaching American History Project*, 5–28.

4 Crossing the Educational Rubicon
Collaboration as a Model for Change

In April 2011, Congress slashed funding for a majority of programs tied to education. Several programs related to professional development for teachers did not survive. While cut severely—from $119 million in Fiscal Year 2010 to $46 million (a loss of $73 million or 61 percent of its funding)— Teaching American History (TAH) grants lived, albeit by their fingertips, another day.[1] Yet, given the economic challenges the United States faces and what appear to be prevailing attitudes in regard to social services and teacher development, it has become clear that history educators cannot rely on federal funding to support efforts to improve the teaching of history.

Nevertheless, meaningful collaboration among K–12 teachers and academic and public historians continues to be vital. This chapter describes in detail the origins and development of a collaborative relationship between a history department and high school in western Michigan. Focusing specifically on four levels of interlocking benefits of collaboration—benefits for high school teachers, for teaching candidates, for high school students, and for historians—the chapter documents the strengths of this collaborative effort and notes areas where purposeful concentration and improvement might benefit all parties. Significantly, the relationship examined here, between WMU's History Department and PCHS, developed without a promise or expectation of financial incentives. It demonstrates that collaboration, while challenging, can survive in the twenty-first century without funding from a TAH grant. The collaboration described in this chapter is focused on again in Part III in terms of a new and ongoing effort to make collaboration the basis for improving students' understanding of the historical discipline.[2]

THE BENEFITS OF COLLABORATION: MULTIPLE PERSPECTIVES

In 2003, Gordon Andrews, a WMU PhD student in history and social studies teacher at nearby PCHS, approached Wilson Warren, professor of history at WMU and the department's history education specialist, about

32 The Current Landscape of History Education

pursuing a TAH grant to bring together WMU's History Department and teachers in the Portage School District. Although the submitted proposal was not funded, discussions about the potential benefits of a joint effort laid the groundwork for subsequent collaborative efforts. The collaborative relationship that emerged focused on various types of interaction between WMU secondary education majors in history and social studies and teachers at Portage Central High School, purposeful interaction among faculty from the respective schools, invitations to teachers to speak to WMU teacher education majors and invitations to historians to speak to the high school students, and greater understanding among faculty about the missions and purposes of history instruction at the secondary and collegiate levels.

FOSTERING A CRAFT APPROACH TO TEACHING HISTORY: COLLABORATION AMONG TEACHERS AND TEACHING CANDIDATES

Placement of student intern teachers in appropriate learning environments is one of the under-discussed dilemmas facing universities and school districts.[3] Like many universities, WMU has faced this problem for many years; there are relatively few districts and teachers who are willing and able to take the fifteen to thirty secondary history and social studies interns in the program each semester, but all candidates need placements as required by state teaching certification requirements. Understandably, part of the reason for this scramble for placements is due to concerns of parents and administrators about who is really teaching their children. As high-stakes assessment dominates the school culture, schools are increasingly reluctant to surrender their students to teaching candidates who are just beginning to experiment with their craft. In the words of Eric Alburtus, principal of PCHS, "almost every year parents comment that they feel like their kids are guinea pigs."[4] Adding to administrative reluctance is the hesitancy of master teachers to become involved due to a host of issues, real or perceived, including the time commitment, potential problems in the classroom, loss over content control, and possible parental/administrative problems.

One of the key aspects of collaboration between WMU and PCHS centers on the improved interaction between teachers and teaching candidates. While the Portage Public School District had previously committed itself to assisting in the preparation of teachers and worked with WMU as a "cluster site," placements had tended to be quite limited. As a result of collaborative efforts, many of the candidates in HIST4940: Teaching Methods for Secondary Schools—a class that is required for all WMU secondary education majors in history and social studies before they intern teach—now either teach a lesson in one of the PCHS social studies classes or have a lesson plan critiqued by a social studies teacher prior to student teaching. Pre-service teachers already participated in a WMU College of Education–administered

Crossing the Educational Rubicon   33

pre-internship experience, but the additional teaching opportunity established as a result of collaboration between the high school and the history department tends to be a much more focused instructional opportunity. Candidates submit a lesson plan that is reviewed by a teacher, who then gives discipline-specific feedback on how the lesson might be taught and what aspects of the lesson might be improved. If the pre-service teacher is given the opportunity to teach a lesson, then the plan serves as the starting point of discussion between the observing teacher and teaching candidate.

Discussing the practice of teaching has benefits for teachers as well as pre-service teachers. A mentor teacher's opportunity to reflect on his or her own craft is invaluable. The pace of the day for any teacher is so rapid that time spent reflecting on the day's lessons is practiced less frequently than one would like to admit. Time dedicated to mentoring a teaching candidate, whether spent in a discussion about a lesson plan or immediately following an observation of the candidate's teaching, can evoke educational dialogues, fruitful not only for the intern who benefits from immediate feedback but also for the master teacher. In a reflective moment, Principal Alburtus noted that "teaching can be a lonely profession and it makes me sad when we see others work in teams, yet in education it is really hard to do . . . A good intern takes those good colleagues and makes them even more comfortable sharing ideas."[5] Responsibility for an intern teacher, then, can serve as a catalyst for the sorts of dialogue that, during those precious few moments throughout the day, can lead to the honing of the craft of teaching.

In addition to providing better experiences for large numbers of pre-service teachers during their practicum, collaborative discussions between Andrews and Warren centered on the student teaching experience. To this end, in 2007 WMU's History Department established the Smith Burnham Outstanding Intern Teacher Award.[6] In creating this award, named after a well-known history educator from WMU, the PCHS's social studies department and administration entered into an agreement with WMU's History Department; each award winner completes the student teaching internship at the school and receives supervision and letters of recommendation from multiple teachers and the school principal.[7] The award has been given each academic semester since fall 2007. Award winners must compete for the honor by submitting application materials and then interviewing with WMU's History Department and PCHS faculty members.

The Smith Burnham program appealed to Dr. Richard Perry, then assistant superintendent for curriculum at Portage Public Schools, particularly because it removed a number of the potentially damaging variables so "you know you are getting an outstanding candidate and you can get this synergy in people working together, and that's what I see as a powerful thing."[8] Because of its competitive nature, the Smith Burnham program places the best WMU intern teacher each semester in PCHS. The school district understands it is getting a superior candidate from the teacher education program at WMU, and this assurance has alleviated some of the building principal's

34 *The Current Landscape of History Education*

and the selected master teacher's reservations. Instrumental to the success of the program, Principal Alburtus, himself a history teacher before embarking on his administrative career, agreed with the tenets of the project and approached Dr. Perry, who recognized the program as a win-win proposition for the district and WMU. The district, Perry reasoned, would be getting highly qualified intern teachers, averring that he didn't "think any member of the community will mistake a low quality individual from a high quality individual."[9]

For Alburtus, the benefits of the program were manifestly positive. He explained, "Some students go into education, particularly at the high school level, because they like the content . . . but don't necessarily work that well with students."[10] Due to the rigorous efforts of the history department to screen candidates who are Smith Burnham winners, some of Alburtus's concerns have been addressed. He recalled crossing paths with a recent Smith Burnham winner on her way to teach a multiweek unit that she had voluntarily undertaken for another teacher, which spoke volumes to him about the sense of dedication these interns have. This type of experience, Alburtus declared, "gives me an overall confidence about the quality of interns coming out of WMU," as the candidates have acquitted themselves well in the classroom and outside of it. [11]

Because placements are so carefully made, the program also offers a guarantee that each intern teacher is placed with a master teacher. This secure placement, as opposed to the all-too-frequent random placement, helps to further underscore a craft approach to the internship. Master teachers and interns are together expected to exchange ideas, develop curriculum, craft lessons, and discuss relevant literature regarding historical thinking and its implementation in the classroom. It has also facilitated the implementation of current pedagogies concerning technology and historical thinking.

Unfortunately, as many students progress through their undergraduate work, they never encounter the types of technologies that are available in many school districts, including Portage. At PCHS, interns are able to utilize a number of new technologies, from smart boards, interactive tablets, and clicker systems, to software that allows them to create their own documentaries and prepare meaningful classroom lessons. All too often, the use of much of this technology is ineffective, perhaps holding students' attention with bells and whistles but leaving looming questions about the extent to which students have engaged in disciplinary thought or used relevant historical habits of mind. As a result of the expectations communicated through creating both the Smith Burnham award and the relationship established between candidates who are methods students and the teachers who critique their work, teachers and candidates sit down and discuss the applications of the best pedagogies and the use of specific technologies to create the most historically relevant lesson. These interactions also reinforce a vital lesson for interns: that teaching history is a purposeful act that must be carefully cultivated to achieve an efficacious end.

The communication that best practice should be a focal point of discussion between teachers and teaching candidates improved collegiality in the social studies department overall, and it facilitated discussions between staff members and Warren. For example, the co-teaching model (between mentor teachers and candidates) is increasingly in use, and it has become quite common to see teachers going in and out of classrooms watching the interns work. On one occasion, as an intern directed a "fishbowl" exercise involving the entire class, several other instructors were drawn to the room. Interested observers included not only Warren but also the mentor teacher, an economics teacher from down the hallway, the head of the department, and another history teacher. This situation created an opportunity to critique the method used in that particular instance, and it fostered further conversations among teachers and the historian about the application of the method in other disciplines. This type of collegiality among teachers and between teachers and university faculty does not exist in every school.

Taking advantage of improved collegial relations and a commitment to their practice, members of PCHS's social studies department have engaged in broader conversations about what it means to teach history. While department meetings generally focus on attending to the bureaucratic details of student distributions, class sizes, class assignments, district assessments, new class proposals, and curricula, the collaborative relationship with WMU and the conversations sparked by consistently working with pre-service teachers has created an occasion for departmental discussions on the topic of pedagogies. Importantly, Warren often participates in these conversations. The administration also takes part in discussions relating to the teaching of history. Having read Sam Wineburg's *Historical Thinking and Other Unnatural Acts* as a result of the collaborative effort between Portage Central teachers and WMU, Alburtus lauded these types of interactions, declaring that "it helps you take more pride in what you are doing, not because you don't have other reasons to be proud of it [the teachers' work] but because it just does! It raises the level of professionalism."[12]

NEWFOUND ENTHUSIASM FOR HISTORY: COLLABORATIVE EFFORTS AND THE IMPACT ON HIGH SCHOOL STUDENTS

In addition to the enhanced internship program, the relationship between Western Michigan University and the teachers at Portage Central has reaped benefits that were not immediately foreseen, and as the relationship matured, other projects flowed from this association. Perhaps sensing their teachers' enthusiasm for the discipline, high school students began to react with increased interest in history as intriguing options presented themselves. Among the achievements associated with the collaborative effort between Portage Central and WMU were the founding of a history club, increased communication between historians and high school students, and

36 The Current Landscape of History Education

the development of an oral history project. In total, the substantive energy and interest created by this program only reinforce the notion that these types of relationships should be encouraged.

As teachers focused increasingly on best practice in history pedagogy and conveyed their enthusiasm to students, one of the first outgrowths of the partnerships was the chartering of the National History Club in 2008 at PCHS with Kent Baker, the social studies department chair at the time and a recipient of the Michigan Council of History Education's Annette and Jim McConnell Secondary History Teacher of the Year Award, as its staff sponsor. The organization itself is user friendly, and at the time Montrose High School was the only school in Michigan with a charter, so it was a great opportunity for students to found a unique club in their region. When students were presented with the idea, they earnestly embraced it, and Portage Central became the second high school in the state to become a member.

Membership provided students with an exceptional opportunity to participate in historical activities. *The Concord Review*, a journal published by the national organization, offered a competitive format for students to submit essays for publication, and is the "only scholarly review of history essays written by secondary students."[13] Since Portage Central is an International Baccalaureate (IB) school, many students write extended essays that fit the structure of the contest, and the incentive of publication inspired non-IB students to participate as well. The National History Club also sponsors an advisor-nominated "history student of the year," and with the strong backing of the school's administration, planned a number of relevant activities. These events included field trips, group discussions, historically based movies, a book club, and guest lecturers.

It was the latter option that sparked a novel idea for the students. The club, taking advantage of the relationship with WMU, solicited history professors from the university to speak. The response from the department was positive, and one of the first historians to visit the campus was Edwin Martini, whose areas of expertise include the Vietnam War, and particularly the wartime use of Agent Orange. Organized by students, this event provided an exciting opportunity as it broadened the audience to include all interested parties. Students prepared for Professor Martini's visit and the promised question-and-answer segment by examining the subject matter on their own.

On the afternoon of the talk, titled, "Cultural Implications of the Vietnam War and American History," the scope of the event was impressive. Attendance exceeded eighty people and included club members and significantly, other members of the social studies department, an administrator, two counselors, librarians, and other PCHS staff. Students and staff members were able to ask questions of Professor Martini, a valuable and unique experience in a high school setting. Martini commented later that many of the students' questions were as good as those offered at the collegiate level. The students' excitement was palpable, and the future opportunities

Crossing the Educational Rubicon 37

for students and staff were eagerly embraced. It was the first of many visits from Western Michigan University historians. Assistant Superintendent Perry mentioned that his sons, upon attending another lecture by a WMU historian, came home newly excited about studying history.[14]

Portage Central students' enthusiasm was certainly a welcome result of having professors visit, and teachers, feeding off students' excitement, were also energized by the university connection. Members of the history club, with the support and coordination of Kent Baker, created an oral history project that focused on interviews with military veterans. The history club students contacted potential interviewees and conducted the interviews. Spurred by students' engagement with the project, teachers solicited the local library to act as a repository for the student-produced oral histories. The library had been involved in the production of oral histories within the community, and the student projects were a natural fit.

WADING INTO UNFAMILIAR TERRAIN: HISTORIANS AND BENEFITS OF COLLABORATION WITH TEACHERS

The benefits to the WMU History Department have also been considerable. As the department's teacher education specialist and main liaison with the area schools, Warren's consistent and long-term dialogue with Andrews and other secondary teacher colleagues provides insights into teachers' concerns that cannot be gained from simply reading professional journals or attending meetings of social studies educators. For instance, the Michigan Department of Education recently promulgated new content expectations for all disciplines that the schools have been busily implementing.[15] World history is now a required subject for all public school students in the state. Discussions with secondary teacher colleagues about their reactions to and problems with the new world history content expectations provide Warren with a better-informed assessment of their benefits and costs. Partly because of these conversations with teachers at PCHS and elsewhere, Warren was able to convince the TAH grant leaders at Kalamazoo Regional Educational Service Agency, with whom he has worked since 2003 on five TAH grants, to use carryover funds from one of the TAH grants to support a workshop on "World History's Impact on U.S. History" for area middle and high school teachers in 2007. The workshop included presentations on several time periods and areas by WMU history faculty. The teachers were also able to ask specific questions regarding the new content expectations. For the historians, examining these expectations and listening to teachers' questions was eye-opening. A similar world history workshop with most of the same WMU history faculty took place in May 2011.

After working with secondary teachers in settings like the world history workshop, WMU History Department faculty now have a much better idea about the issues and concerns of their colleagues in the schools. This direct

38   The Current Landscape of History Education

exposure to teachers' ideas and concerns enhances Warren's efforts to convey teachers' perspectives when discussing issues relevant to the preparation of WMU's secondary education majors with his History Department colleagues. As a department in an institution that teaches thousands of future K–12 educators, it is essential that faculty have firsthand information about developments in the schools. Partly because the Michigan Department of Education demands it, WMU's History Department must continuously revise its curriculum for future secondary teachers to meet new state mandates. It makes little sense for historians to make curricular changes based merely on a list from the state. Rather, it is imperative to hear from colleagues in the schools about how these changes may or may not make a positive impact on the schools' curriculum and instruction.[16] Because of the relationship between Portage Central High School and the WMU History Department, historians have begun to engage in deeper conversations about course offerings and ways to best prepare history teachers to use the content and methods of the discipline with high school students. In this regard, the WMU-Portage Central collaboration has parallels to similar efforts associated with TAH programs.[17]

CONTINUOUS WORK IN COLLABORATION

The collaborative spirit that exists between the teachers and historians at Portage Central High School and Western Michigan University provides an opportunity for further discussions in areas that have remained untapped. Two such areas are teaching for historical thinking and craft-based approaches to historical instruction and assessment of student learning. Both are increasing areas of concern for high school history teachers and historians.

During the 2005–2006 school year, the social studies department at Portage Central began a best practices self-study. Participants conducted interviews with students about their understanding of the discipline of history, and they interviewed fellow teachers in regard to their understanding of what history is. After combining these understandings with current research in history education, members of the department began to discuss various approaches to fostering historical thinking. Unfortunately, because of lack of funding the study never moved beyond these initial discussions. While working with teaching candidates provides teachers with the opportunity to discuss "why I used this source or asked this question as opposed to that source or that question," teachers also need to have these conversations among themselves, and historians should be present for the discussion. Given the recent interest of many historians in the scholarship of teaching and learning and the push in higher education to document assessments, it would seem that the established collaboration between Portage Central teachers and WMU historians could be used to renew and push forward discussions about teaching and learning in history. Historians can lend their expertise in regard to domain-specific concepts and disciplinary ways of knowing; teachers can contribute their experience in working with various learners, their skills in teaching, and their familiarity with assessment. Too often the emphasis at both the high school level and university level has been on "getting the historical part right" in a history class. As many TAH initiatives have also stressed, the time has come for historians and history teachers to emphasize historical thinking in every teaching act and to communicate to students from the outset that while facts matter, history is about bringing meaning to facts through the interpretation of evidence.[18]

The development of effective history instructional and assessment practices is another area in which the collaborative effort between WMU and Portage Central might focus its energies in the future. Increasingly in Michigan, and elsewhere, school districts, sometimes in cooperation with state departments of education, have transferred curriculum and assessment from those most knowledgeable about the discipline—the historians—and those who possess pedagogical content knowledge—the teachers. This is evidenced by the increasing number of canned curricula or classes on a computer that reduce teaching to a process, effectively removing the teacher from the equation. Instead, teachers become the delivery mechanisms following the requisite steps, with the outcomes measured in a series of nauseating quizzes, tests, and district assessments, both formal and informal, throughout the week. In states like Michigan there is a push toward online courses that mimic the old Skinnerian model, which moves students from one unit to the next, or the use of a "blended curriculum," as in the Grand Rapids Public Schools, which follows a three-day rotation. On day one the teacher reads a script to students, on day two students complete a five-panel PowerPoint answering a question related to the script topic, and day three requires students to answer a new question or complete the question from the day before. Students then return to day one, the teacher is handed a script, and the process begins again.[19] Reasons for the removal of a craft approach over that of process include a mix of political, educational, and economic policies that ignore years of research. What we can learn from the WMU-Portage Central collaboration, as well as many of the TAH programs over the past decade, is that professionals allowed to labor at the craft of teaching history enrich our students' lives through continued education, deep passion for the scholarship of teaching and learning history, and the successful creation of imaginative and historically authentic lessons.[20]

BRIDGING THE EDUCATIONAL RUBICON

Although Gordon Andrews left Portage Central for Grand Valley State University in the fall of 2009, the Smith Burnham program has continued with Tama Salisbury as its Portage Central coordinator. On the whole, the

40   The Current Landscape of History Education

program has offered both direct and indirect benefits to the district, teachers, interns, community, and students, as well as WMU's History Department. This begs the question, why aren't more of these relationships in existence? The fact of the matter is that money and its availability tend to occupy the attention of most school districts when it comes to fostering institutional relationships. Most recently for history, that has been exemplified through the distribution of monies through the auspices of the TAH. Programs like the Smith Burnham Outstanding Intern Award offer opportunities for both collegiate and K–12 institutions to come together in a collegial fashion without the strictures of financing. Freed from the hindrance that money often presents, two entities that share so many interests and objectives need not be separated by a formidable and unbridgeable Rubicon.

The relationship between WMU and Portage Central has served as the creative impetus for teachers, historians, and students to come together in ways that are too often overlooked. The interlocking benefits of collaboration, specifically those for high school teachers and historians, described in this essay have also been achieved in many places in the country through the TAH program. Indeed, collaboration among a wide array of teachers, history and education faculty, and public historians has been arguably the crowning achievement of the TAH program. Perhaps most distinctive about the WMU and Portage Central effort compared to the TAH program has been its focus on collaboration among high school teachers and historians for the purpose of helping teacher candidates, at both the pre-intern and intern levels. The TAH program has generally had only indirect benefits for prospective teachers. High school students have also been more direct beneficiaries of the WMU-Portage Central collaboration than has been true in many cases with the TAH program.

The WMU and Portage Central collaborative partnership is also instructive in terms of the funding issue. Collaborations need not involve large infusions of capital in the traditional sense or require hours of grant writing and hand wringing, with hope for the acquisition of money that will certainly run out and leave districts in a continuous hunt for more. What this partnership demonstrates is the myriad positive results that can occur from the appropriate use of human capital toward creating energized historical communities. Just as the forums in the Portage Central media center provided a unique opportunity for students, staff, and historians to consider history together, so too, WMU and Portage Central's collaborative effort allowed teachers and historians a unique opportunity to use current historiography and pedagogy as part of a vibrant historical conversation.

In the end, the result has been an ever-widening appreciation for the place of history in our students' and teachers' lives that benefits the broader community. Through their participation in oral history projects and the creation of historical organizations like the history club, students learn that an understanding of history is necessary to become an informed citizen. Likewise, teachers have had the opportunity to participate in the kind of teaching and learning experiences that serve as a meaningful model of professional development. Professors have gained a better appreciation of the teachers' content and pedagogical challenges. Since this collaborative model stems from mutual interests and concerns for history education and was never dependent on monetary support, its collaborators have the luxury of focusing their energies on enhancing their relationship without worrying about whether or not the funding stream will run dry.

Collaboration works best when all parties share mutual interests and concerns. Certainly the money provided with the TAH program has facilitated conversations, but long-term collaboration requires more than money. Andrews and Warren discovered over the years in their frequent conversations, including those that took place in hour-long car rides to and from Lansing for Michigan Council for History Education board meetings, that they share mutual concerns about many aspects of history as a profession and how history is conveyed to students. When educators invoke the notion of "seamless" K–16 education, this seems impossible to achieve on any large-scale level. But it seems realistic in more limited dimensions when it is based on long-term personal interactions among secondary school teachers and academics.

NOTES

Please note that this essay was originally published as Gordon Andrews, Wilson J. Warren, Sarah Drake Brown, "Crossing the Educational Rubicon without the TAH: Collaboration among University and Secondary-Level History Educators," *The History Teacher* 46:2(2013), 253–66.

1. "History Programs Make Major Cuts in FY '11 Federal Budget." http://historycoalition.org/2011/04/13/history-programs-face-major-cuts-in-fy-11-federal-budget/ (accessed on April 30, 2011). For a generally laudatory scholarly assessment of the Teaching American History Program, see Rachel G. Ragland and Kelly A. Woestman, eds., *The Teaching American History Project: Lessons for History Educators and Historians* (New York: Routledge, 2009). Although his comments are not focused on problems with TAH-sponsored collaboration, Sam Wineburg recently questioned the program's effectiveness because of missing or inconsistent evaluation data. See Rick Shenkman, "OAH 2009: Sam Wineburg Dares to Ask If the Teaching American History Program Is a Boondoogle," *History News Network*, April 20, 2009, http://hnn.us/articles/76806.html (accessed January 2, 2011).
2. David Wrobel's essay on the benefits of collaboration between K–12 and academic historians challenges academics, in particular, to think about the benefits beyond TAH funding. See "A Lesson from the Past and Some Hope for the Future: The History Academy and the Schools, 1880–2007," *The History Teacher* 41:2(2008), 151–62. For other recent reflections on the value of collaboration in history education, see, for example, Patricia Cleary and David Neumann, "The Challenges of Primary Sources, Collaboration, and the K-16 Elizabeth Murray Project," *The History Teacher* 43:1(2009), 67–86; Rachel G. Ragland, "Changing Secondary Teachers' Views of Teaching American

42 The Current Landscape of History Education

History," *The History Teacher* 40:2(2007), 219–46; Kelly Ann Long, "Reflections on TAH and the Historian's Role: Reciprocal Exchanges and Transformative Contributions to History Education," *The History Teacher* 39:4(2006), 493–508; and Kenneth T. Jackson, "The Power of History: The Weakness of a Profession," *Journal of American History* 88:4(2002), 1299–314. The collaborative relationships explained in this essay suggest that Linda Symcox's argument in "Forging New Partnerships: Collaboration between University Professors and Classroom Teachers to Improve History Teaching, 1983–2011," *The History Teacher* 45:3(May 2012), 359–82, that partnerships require substantial funding is not valid. Her perspectives rest on a model, often encouraged by Teaching American History projects, that predicated collaboration on elite historians being brought in at great expense for short-term professional development.

3. See, for instance, Robert V. Bullough, Jr., "Teacher Vulnerability and Teachability: A Case Study of a Mentor and Two Interns," *Teacher Education Quarterly* 32:2(2005), 23–39; Edwin G. Ralph, "Interns' and Cooperating Teachers' Concerns during the Extended Practicum," *Alberta Journal of Educational Research* 50:4(2004), 411–29; and Sandra K. Abell, Deborah R. Dillon, Carol J. Hopkins, William D. McInerney, and David G. O'Brien, "'Somebody to Count On': Mentor/Intern Relationships in a Beginning Teacher Internship Program," *Teaching and Teacher Education* 11:2 (1995), 173–88.

4. Eric Alburtus, interview with Gordon Andrews, October 29, 2009, digital tape in Andrews's possession.

5. Ibid.

6. From 1919 to 1939, Smith Burnham was chair of Western State Normal School's Department of History and Social Science. In 1927, Western State Normal School was renamed Western State Teachers College, before it then became Western Michigan University in 1957. Between 1918 and 1934, Burnham published six textbooks on U.S. history aimed at both elementary and secondary school audiences. His textbooks emphasized critical thinking and problem-solving perspectives. Burnham was also a tireless public speaker. In addition to speeches for educator audiences, he gave hundreds of speeches to various community groups in Michigan and the Midwest. On Burnham's career, see, Wilson J. Warren, "The Evolution of a History-Centered Teaching Program: Western Michigan University's Preparation of Secondary Teachers," in *History Education 101: The Past, Present, and Future of Teacher Preparation*, ed., Wilson J. Warren and D. Antonio Cantu (Charlotte, NC: Information Age Publishing, Inc., 2008), 48–50.

7. Beginning with the spring 2012 award, each recipient also received $250 from the History Department.

8. Richard Perry, interview with Gordon Andrews, January 15, 2010, digital tape in Andrews' possession.

9. Alburtus, interview.

10. Ibid.

11. Ibid.

12. Ibid.

13. Information regarding the founding of a National History Club charter can be found at http://www.nationalhistoryclub.org (accessed January 15, 2011). Information regarding *The Concord Review* can be found at http://www.tcr.org (accessed July 16, 2015).

14. Perry, interview.

15. The Michigan High School Social Studies Content Expectations can be found at: http://www.michigan.gov/documents/mde/SS_HSCE_9–15–09_292358_7.pdf (accessed January 15, 2011).

Crossing the Educational Rubicon   43

16. Evidence of Western Michigan University's History Department's efforts to work with secondary school colleagues, and improve its undergraduate and graduate curriculum, can be found in the following articles: James R. Palmitessa, "Retention of Doctoral Students," *Perspectives* 45:9(2007), 27–28; Wilson J. Warren, "Bridging the Gap between K–12 Teachers and Postsecondary Historians," *Perspectives on History* 46:7(2008), 52–54; and Linda J. Borish, Mitch Kachun, and Cheryl Lyon-Jenness, "Rethinking a Curricular "Muddle in the Middle": Revising the Undergraduate History Major at Western Michigan University." *Journal of American History* 95:4(2009), 1102–13.

17. The Teaching American History program has achieved considerable success in regard to making history professors better aware of the range of abilities, skills, concerns, and limitations of elementary and secondary history teachers. To some degree, these insights have also been applied to efforts aimed at modifying and improving how history is taught at the collegiate level. For an insightful survey of some of the TAH program's benefits for history professors, see Peter B. Knupfer, "A New Focus for the History Professoriate: Professional Development for History Teachers as Professional Development for Historians," in *The Teaching American History Project*, 29–46.

18. The Teaching American History program has made considerable strides in alerting elementary, secondary, and collegiate history teachers to the scholarship of teaching and learning, particularly in terms of areas such as best practices in teaching and student engagement, pedagogical content knowledge, and collaborative methods. See, for instance, Rachel G. Ragland, "*Teaching American History* Projects in Illinois: A Comparative Analysis of Professional Development Models," in *The Teaching American History Project*, 163–201; and Ann Marie Ryan and Frank Valadez, "Designing and Implementing Content-Based Professional Development for Teachers of American History," in *The Teaching American History Project*, 216–239.

19. On "blended curriculum," see, for example, Brigid Schulte, "Hybrid Schools for the iGeneration," *Education Digest* 77:1(2011), 22–26; and Katie Ash, "Curricula All Over Map for 'Blended' Classes," *Education Week* 30:15(January 12, 2011), Supp. 5-Supp. 7. On the Grand Rapids blended curriculum context, see Kym Reinstadler, "Grand Rapids Public Schools Hopes Online Courses Will Boost Poor Graduation Rate," *Grand Rapids Press* (online), April 30, 2010 (accessed October 13, 2011); and Katie Ash, "Hybrid versus Online in K–12," *SOETalk*, January 14, 2011, http://soetalk.com/2011/01/14/hybrid-versus-online-in-K–12/ (accessed October 13, 2011).

20. For a powerful expression of how the TAH program has motivated teachers to pursue craft-based approaches to effective history teaching, see Kelly A. Woestman, "Teachers as Historians: A Historian's Experiences with TAH Projects," in *The Teaching American History Project*, 5–28.

Part II

The Argument for Creating the Space to Think and Teach Historically

The Gilder Lehrman Institute of American History's National History Teacher of the Year program annually recognizes elementary and secondary history teachers who have honed their craft in the way that this book champions. In the current landscape of history education, the Gilder Lehrman Institute stands out for its various initiatives, including not only the History Teacher of the Year program but also its library collections, programs, exhibits, and online materials, among other resources, that support teachers' professional development in a way that embodies the important elements of the historian's craft. This portion of the book highlights how the History Teacher of the Year winners have been able to create the space to think and teach historically in their own professional careers and their classrooms. Their professional and classroom concerns serve as a model for craft-based teaching. First and foremost, the award winners approach their classroom efforts in a way that stresses development of students' historical thinking. The award selection process also embodies a collaborative evaluation approach that is offered as a counterpoint to the current focus on "best practices" systems for teacher evaluation throughout the profession.

5 Developing a Craft Approach to Teaching History

What We Can Learn from the Gilder Lehrman Institute of American History's National History Teachers of the Year

The Gilder Lehrman Institute of American History's National History Teachers of the Year (HTOY) program supports and rewards teachers who pursue their careers as a craft. HTOY recipients share an approach to the teaching of history that provides insightful solutions to some of the most pressing problems facing history education. Examining how these teachers implement their craft draws attention to various conceptions of the role of the teacher, provides suggestions related to teacher preparation and development, and offers insights into the vexing problem of evaluating what good history teaching looks like. The HTOY program highlights teachers who hone discipline-specific skills and approach their work as teacher-scholars. This chapter draws attention to curricular constraints imposed on teachers, examines the work of teachers who have successfully resisted these constraints, and places their work in the larger context of the purposes of history education.

With school districts around the country scrambling to increase test scores to escape punitive measures mandated by No Child Left Behind, educational Taylorism has increasingly replaced the craft of teaching, to the detriment of students. At the turn of the twentieth-century Frederick W. Taylor developed techniques that reduced skilled applications in manufacturing to their simplest form, creating efficiency models (deskilling), which allowed workers to perform one task more quickly throughout the day. This lowered costs, raised profits, and led to the pursuit of the "'one best way', to do a job."[1] The current trend to test, test, and test some more runs contrary to the findings of Jonathan Rees, S. G. Grant, and others who have documented not only the negative impact of testing on the practices of teachers in the classroom but also, in the case of Grant, the absence of any evidence that reform, based on testing, has succeeded. Rees asserted, "Scientific management in the classroom does not respect the idea that teachers know what to teach their students or how best to teach it."[2]

To be fair, this emphasis on process over craft in the realm of education has been evolving for decades, because the advent of "best practices" studies identified skills and techniques that teachers could use in the classroom to elevate learning across content areas and the concurrent push for charter

48   *Argument for the Space to Think and Teach*

schools.[3] Examples of best practices include cooperative learning, the use of varied instructional techniques, and multiple intelligences.[4] When used by teachers pursuing their disciplinary craft, these methods can be fruitful. However, the trend has been to divorce the craft of teaching from the classroom in favor of curricular process.[5]

The move toward educational Taylorism is found in the increasing number of canned curriculums or classes on a computer that reduce teaching to a process that removes the teacher from the equation.[6] Teachers become delivery mechanisms. Their success is measured in a series of quizzes, tests, and district assessments. The term often used for these types of curriculum packages is *teacher-proofed*, and they are effectively a management system put in place to remove teachers from the equation (as much as possible) to raise test scores.[7] In states like Michigan, there is a push toward online courses that mimic the Skinnerian model, which moves students from one unit to the next, or the use of a blended curriculum, which follows a three-day scripted progression.[8]

Unfortunately, curricular and pedagogical decisions are being taken out of the hands of teachers, impeding the effective use of content pedagogy in the classroom.[9] Each of the Gilder Lehrman National History Teachers of the Year demonstrates that professionals allowed to practice the craft of teaching history enrich our students' lives through continued education, a deep passion for history education, and successful creation of imaginative and historically authentic lessons. The Gilder Lehrman Institute for American History's HTOY commends those teachers who have nurtured teaching as a craft.

What does it mean to cultivate a craft? It means many things, including reading widely, seeking out others in the field, creating organizational affiliations, experimenting, risking failure, and certainly pursuing excellence in the best tradition of the scholar-teacher. It also assumes the continuous pursuit of knowledge, both formally and informally, in the discipline of history. The Gilder Lehrman Institute was established in 1994 to promote "the study and love of American History" and accomplishes its mission with an impressive array of interactions among historians, teachers, and the public. By sponsoring national book awards, summer institutes for teachers, and professional development, as well as granting access to primary documents from its private holdings, fellowships, and lectures by distinguished historians in the field of American History, the institute has established itself as one of the preeminent U.S. history organizations in the country.[10]

Recognized teachers are selected from the ranks of elementary and secondary educators annually and are nominated by colleagues, students, administrators, or the parents of students. These teachers provide curriculum vitae, a statement of teaching philosophy, letters of recommendation from those who have witnessed their teaching, evidence of student success, and a sample lesson accompanied by a video explanation. The Gilder Lehrman verifies their eligibility, and then their work is sent to the state

A Craft Approach to Teaching History 49

coordinators who vet the nominees and select a representative from their particular state or territory.

THE NATIONAL WINNERS

Studies exist that identify successful teacher traits or scrutinize what teachers do in the classroom.[11] However, most teachers are never assessed by experts in their field; most will be visited by a principal whose chief concern, according to recent data, is not with the teacher's content knowledge but rather classroom management and techniques to help struggling students.[12] In either case, principals are the curricular leaders who evaluate the professional effectiveness of teachers in their building. States, like New York, are nudging the bar even lower with the establishment of "leadership academies," where professionals with degrees—many of whom have never taught—will be turned into principals in a short time and allowed to lead schools.[13] The Gilder Lehrman Institute provides a model of teacher assessment that is evidenced in the HTOY. Candidates for the HTOY are nominated online and then vetted by the Gilder Lehrman to make sure applicants have met all the requirements.[14] Qualified candidates are forwarded to the Gilder Lehrman's state coordinators and selected according to the criteria. For example, in Michigan the state coordinator is a member of the Michigan Council for History Education (MCHE), and there is a vote by the board to secure the winner. For the sake of full disclosure, Gordon Andrews has served as the state coordinator for the past decade. What follows is based on his experiences and interviews with HTOY winners. Each of the winners understands that continuing his or her formal education necessarily includes attaining an advanced degree in a content area.[15]

Like many nominees, Rosanne Lichatin, the 2005 teacher of the year, has pursued an advanced degree in her content area at great personal expense and sacrifice. She earned a bachelor's degree in history from Kean University, a master's degree in history from East Stroudsburg in Pennsylvania, and an additional forty-five credits in graduate-level history courses. When asked why she had engaged in extensive historical study, she responded that the more you learn "the more you are aware of what you don't know." It is that self-awareness and passion for the discipline that drives her to continue her own learning, and that passion is certainly transferred to her students.[16] David Mitchell, the 2008 winner from Massachusetts, possesses two master's degrees involving history, and 2010 winner, Nathan (Nate) McAlister, who teaches in Kansas, obtained a master of arts in teaching (MAT) that also focuses on history. He felt compelled to pursue his degree after he started teaching to cultivate a greater understanding of history in a purposeful effort to compensate for what he felt was weak preparation and to be the best teacher possible to his students.[17]

50 Argument for the Space to Think and Teach

In stark contrast, Arne Duncan, secretary of education, in a speech to the American Enterprise Institute on November 17, 2010, informed the audience that they should use fiscally difficult times "as an opportunity to make dramatic improvements." One of the "opportunities" he outlined is an end to increased salaries for teachers who obtain a master's degree. Duncan informed the audience that "there is little evidence teachers with masters degrees improve student achievement more than other teachers—with the possible exception of teachers who earn masters in math and science." Over the past twenty years, a consistent body of evidence has confirmed findings that well-prepared teachers outperform less-well-prepared teachers in content areas, grudgingly alluded to by the secretary of education.[18] Some, like Duncan, argue that economic constraints should be used to de-skill the profession of teaching by discounting master's degrees, but the evidence belies these assertions as nothing but a straw man erected to diminish the craft. As Linda Darling-Hammond has succinctly stated, teachers need to know "subject matter deeply and flexibly."[19]

What drives the Gilder Lehrman's national winners to continue striving within the craft? Rosanne Lichatin, who is now an education coordinator for two of the Gilder Lehrman summer seminars, as well as a classroom teacher in her thirty-sixth year of teaching, pointed to an inspiring meeting with other winners, brought together by Dr. James Basker, president of the Gilder Lehrman Institute. During the meeting, winners discussed significant aspects of their teaching and what the award meant to them personally and professionally. One observation Lichatin shared was the profound respect they had for their profession, commenting that "each cares deeply about their teaching and each cares deeply about their kids." That deep respect and concern is evidenced in the way these teachers approach not only their own professional education but also the way they approach their lessons.

Teachers selected by the Gilder Lehrman present their students with personally crafted lessons that purposefully involve their students in the disciplinary aspects of history, commonly referred to as historical thinking. Nathan McAlister stated that he wanted his students to be able to think critically about the issues that have confronted the people of the United States throughout our history. In her acceptance speech, Maureen Festi, the 2005 elementary winner, expressed her philosophy to the audience eloquently.

> I have discovered that fifth grade journeys into the past need to be more than the memorization of facts from textbooks. Students need to touch and be touched by history. They touch history when they take on the roles of historians and interact with primary historical information. As they experience it, think about it, question it, challenge it, and make meaningful connections to their everyday lives, they begin to develop an American identity. They need to grab onto history, grapple with it, and make it their own.[20]

A Craft Approach to Teaching History 51

So, what does that look like in the classroom? How do master teachers craft lessons that challenge their students to think historically?

IMPLEMENTING STRATEGIES IN THE CLASSROOM

The HTOY winners consistently develop engaging lessons and learning opportunities that require students to think deeply about history and demonstrate what they have learned in a way that is disciplinarily relevant.[21] To enable their students to understand the complexities of history, master teachers spend long hours planning. They understand that historically literate citizens are better able to understand their own lives within the grand scheme of human and societal development. To that end, they take great pride, and suffer a considerable amount of angst, over how best to make the sometimes intricate and nuanced complexities of U.S. history intellectually palatable yet challenging for each class. Interestingly, because of their disciplinary expertise these teachers are able to perform distinct tasks with their students utilizing sources that many teachers fail to consider or understand.

In his research on the connection between curriculum and instruction, Avner Segall draws a subtle but important distinction when it comes to considering the pedagogical quality of texts. Segall suggests that when it comes to content knowledge, "it has not addressed the need for teachers to examine the inherently instructional aspects of content and what that examination might entail for their practice as classroom teachers."[22] Versed in the disciplinary distinctions of sources, however, HTOY winners are able to glean from texts their silences vis-à-vis issues of race, gender, and ethnicity, evaluating those sources as to their instructional quality as Segall suggests. Because of their commitment to professional development that is discipline-oriented, they have become attuned to textual and intertextual continuities and discontinuities that allow them to routinely make use of the pedagogical opportunities presented by sources. And as a result, they are able to create an engaged learning environment.

Responding to a question on how she approaches the preparation of a lesson, Rosanne Lichatin was insightful.

> Each individual history lesson is part of a larger unit of study. At the beginning of a unit I identify an essential question that will guide each of my lessons, and typically, that question becomes the essay question students will respond to at the end of the unit. An essential question is generally a broad one that is open ended. Each individual lesson builds on the foundation of the essential question. For each unit, I identify the *core documents* that my students should be exposed to, and I search for those that give particular insight into the lives of ordinary Americans as well. These documents become the basis of our class discussion.

52 *Argument for the Space to Think and Teach*

> I ask students to read documents "closely." That is, in addition to answering teacher-designed questions which typically ask for historical context, time, author, audience, purpose, validity, and tone, I ask that they focus their attention on the language and details of the document. Unfamiliar words should be defined, and the document should be underlined in key places and show lots of analysis in the margins. Of course, primary sources may also include paintings, posters, maps, broadsides, artifacts, etc. I employ a number of tools to analyze various forms of primary sources. The questions guide the lesson. The primary sources are the "meat" of the lesson. And, the discussion that is generated from the primary sources allows students the opportunity to master the art of analysis and argument.[23]

These teachers demonstrate imagination as well as historical and pedagogical expertise. Nathan McAlister utilized his graduate degree and his continued participation in Teaching American History Projects, as well as the Gilder Lehrman's summer institutes, in a unit on the Civil War. He had his students reenact battles out on the school grounds, nurturing a sense of historical empathy that no textbook could emulate. One of Maureen Festi's many lessons for her fifth-grade students involved hands-on investigation of a colonial ironworks, a far cry from typical upper-elementary experiences. Whereas technology clearly has a role in her classroom, aiding her students' research, it does not end there. The lesson required these ten- and eleven-year-olds to use primary sources, compasses, maps, and local sites to unearth the existence of the mill and analyze its impact, "leaving," she said, "far more questions than answers."[24] David Mitchell, of Whitman-Hanson Regional High School in Massachusetts, uses debate, fishbowls, and primary sources, including "documents, photos, cartoons, and letters," to encourage his students to think more deeply about history. He said this helps his students feel "the pulse of history."[25]

Michele Anderson, 2014 HTOY, teaches at John Glenn High School for the Wayne Westland Community Schools in Michigan. She, too, has completed an MA in history. Her award-winning project was a "World War II Oral History and USO Dance Project." The project allowed her students to conduct interviews with veterans, secure releases, thoroughly research secondary sources, and ultimately submit their interview to the Library of Congress. Because of her disciplinary approach, Michele's students are able to participate in securing history for future generations. Not only have they secured participant voices for the future, but they have also enriched their own lives by understanding the challenges and triumphs of the people who served in WWII. Michele's students are allowed to immerse themselves in history. This is what master teachers bring to their students on a daily basis, enriching their lives in both measurable and immeasurable ways, and cultivating a mature understanding of history that will inform their adult lives.[26]

WHAT CAN WE LEARN?

The current trend in educational Taylorism is anathema to good teaching. It is clearly eschewed by the HTOY winners. We learn from the national award winners the importance of preparation and development, teacher assessment, and the possibilities that may be realized when a professional is permitted to labor in the craft. With regard to teacher preparation and professional development, content matters. A good deal has been written about the Finnish success story of late, and Pasi Sahlberg in *Finnish Lessons* points out that all of Finland's teachers possess a master's degree before entering the classroom.[27] The old axiom that "you can't teach what you don't know" is taken seriously by the world's leading educational system. In turn, this should aid our universities in understanding the vital importance of creating graduate degree options for teachers in the field. For example, most teachers do not plan on entering doctoral programs and are discouraged from degree programs that have language, thesis, and oral defense requirements. In contrast, a master of arts in teaching offers the same rigorous graduate content as the MA, including classes on pedagogy, that are essential in effective K–12 teaching. The HTOY winners are examples of the varied needs of history teachers in the field; universities must address those needs by offering both degrees within their graduate history departments.

The American Historical Association has long advocated meaningful and substantive professional development for K–12 teachers, and the HTOY clearly seek out content-specific professional development.[28] The nominated teachers demonstrate their preference for relevant content through their experiences in Teaching American History Projects, National Endowment for the Humanities programs, and participation in the Gilder Lehrman's summer institutes. Not only do the professional development opportunities offer welcome and appreciated content knowledge but also substantial occasions for discussing pedagogy. The Gilder Lehrman's summer institutes, for example, culminate in lessons created by teachers in a collaborative fashion that they can take back to their districts and implement in their own classrooms. These experiences could, and need to be, replicated in school districts. The cost is nominal when one considers the hundreds of thousands of dollars spent by districts on canned curricula. Instead districts could unlock the synergistic intellectual capital of their teachers and produce rich, historically relevant educational experiences for their students at a fraction of the cost.

Professional development of the type advocated here influenced McAlister. As he progressed toward his master's degree, McAlister contemplated "how to get students involved, and that evolved into, how do I get the students to think like historians?"[29] This reflection moved him quickly away from a "chapter, worksheet" format (mimicking his student teaching experience), as he realized that was not the way he wanted to teach. Lichatin

54   Argument for the Space to Think and Teach

too recounted, "My approach has definitely changed over the years as a result of the Teaching American History grants and the seminars (Gilder Lehrman) I have attended. When I first started teaching I had a sense of the value of primary sources, but I did not know how to access them in ways that would work in the classroom."[30] HTOY winners are continually working to improve their teaching, seeking out content-rich professional development.

Assessing what master history teachers do in the classroom is also an area in which the Gilder Lehrman's HTOY process can help inform the broader K–12 community. Theirs is a collaborative effort—rarely emulated in the K–12 world. Teachers participating in the process spoke of the respect they gained for the excellent teaching that occurs across the nation at all levels. They were also impressed with the way the reviewers were able to hone in on common understandings of which prospective teachers emerged as finalists. After reviewing candidates individually, they then confer as a group, routinely identifying the same teachers as finalists, then through extensive collaboration agreeing on the winner.[31] Teachers are rarely, if ever, evaluated by anyone in their content area, and if an administrator does have the content, the odds that they taught long enough or well enough to be considered a master teacher are smaller yet. However, a collegial environment within which master teachers and historians discuss what good teaching looks like in order to improve pedagogy need not be a utopian dream. It would take a greater degree of trust than now exists in the country for teachers, broadly speaking, and the encouragement of universities toward their faculty to engage in service with public schools. Conversations surrounding pedagogy commonly take place in the GLI summer seminars, where teachers and historians are able to discuss conversationally the discipline and delivery of history content. This is a model worth pursuing.[32]

We also learn from the HTOY winners that to teach history as a craft is to labor in a particular fashion that needs to be encouraged. Laboring within the discipline is common among the winners, providing them with a wisdom that comes from a lifetime's examination of what it means to teach history. In turn, that wisdom allows them countless opportunities to impart their own love and appreciation of history to their students. Equally important to the notion of a craft is the freedom to toil daily in an effort to continually create the best lessons possible for their students. Great teachers create; they are not handed a script, and they do not use a canned curriculum. Instead, they labor to enhance the craft and thus the lives of their students. They would no more read a script than an artist would use a paint-by-numbers kit.

In the late 1980s, amid a tumultuous debate over history in the schools, Paul Gagnon and the Bradley Commission argued for the place of history in American schools by publishing *Historical Literacy: The Case for History In American Education*. In it, various historians argued forcefully and elegantly over pedagogy and content, but perhaps most importantly they

A Craft Approach to Teaching History   55

detailed the myriad ways the study of history expands our understanding of the world and our place in it. In one passage, the historian Gordon Craig pointed to eighteenth-century writer Friedrich Schiller, "History, in so far as it accustoms human beings to comprehend the whole of the past and to hasten forward with its conclusions into the far future, conceals the boundaries of birth and death, which enclose the life of the human being so narrowly and oppressively, and with a kind of optical illusion, expands his short existence into endless space, leading the individual imperceptibly over into humanity."[33]

By providing lessons that require students to think historically, the HTOY winners bring students closer to a substantial understanding of history. It is difficult to imagine the condition movingly described by Schiller accomplished by teachers consigned to a facile process.

NOTES

Please note that this essay was originally published as Gordon Andrews, "Developing a Craft Approach in History Teaching: What We Can Learn from the Gilder Lehrman Institute of American History's National Teachers of the Year," *Teaching History: A Journal of Methods* 39:2(2014), 91–102.

1. Jonathan Rees, "Frederick Taylor in the Classroom: Standardized Testing and Scientific Management," *Radical Pedagogy* 3:2(2001). http://radicalpedagogy. icap.org/content/issue3.2 (accessed May 3, 2013).
2. Ibid.
3. Andrew J. Wayne and Peter Youngs, "Teacher Characteristics and Student Achievement Gains: A Review," *Review of Educational Research* 73:1(2003), 89–122.
4. William A. Owings and Leslie S. Kaplan, ed., *Best Practices, Best Thinking, and Emerging Issues in School Leadership* (Thousand Oaks, CA: Corwin Press, 2003), 72.
5. Although his article is primarily focused on assessment issues, Sam Wineburg's "Beyond 'Breadth and Depth': Subject Matter Knowledge and Assessment," *Theory into Practice* 36:4(1997), 255–61, is an important reminder that there are no truly generalizable thinking skills, only disciplinary-based thinking skills.
6. *Bring Learning Alive: The TCI Approach for Middle and High School Social Studies* (Palo Alto, CA: Teachers' Curriculum Institute, 2004). On increased computer usage, see the International Association for Online Learning where the organization points out that there are forty states with some type of online opportunity and thirty states with fulltime online schools that were used to instruct some 1,816,400 students in 2009–2010, *International Association for Online Learning*, "Key K–12 Online Learning Stats." http://www.inacol.org (accessed July 11, 2012).
7. Linda Darling-Hammond, "Teacher Learning that Supports Student Learning," in *Teaching For Intelligence*, ed. Barbara Z. Presseisen (Thousand Oaks, CA: Corwin Press, 2003), Second Ed., 91–93.
8. Gordon Andrews, Field Notes, Union High School, Grand Rapids Public Schools, February 17, 2011.

56 Argument for the Space to Think and Teach

9. Avner Segall, "What Is the Connection between Curriculum and Instruction," in *Social Studies Today: Research and Practice*, ed. Walter C. Parker (New York: Routledge, 2010), 227.

10. Gilder Lehrman Institute of American History's Mission Statement, http://www.gilderlehrman.org/institute/ (accessed April 3, 2013).

11. Teacher traits have been examined over the years. Some of the noteworthy studies include Martin Haberman, *Star Teachers of Children in Poverty* (West Lafayette, IN: Kappa Delta Pi, 1995); Sam Wineburg's *Historical Thinking and Other Unnatural Acts: Charting the Future of Teaching the Past* (Philadelphia: Temple University Press, 2001); and *Social Studies Today: Research and Practice*, ed. Walter C. Parker, all of which provide insights into what teachers need to know as well as successful common traits.

12. Jean Johnson, "The Principal's Priority 1," *Educational Leadership* 66:1(2008), 72–76.

13. Diane Ravitch, *The Death and Life of the Great American School System* (New York: Basic Books, 2010), 72.

14. For a closer examination of the selection criteria please see the Gilder Lehrman website where eligibility and the selection process, and teacher requirements are outlined. http://www.gilderlehrman.org/programs-exhibitions/eligibility (accessed August 13, 2013).

15. Michigan Department of Education Office of Professional Preparation Services: Facts On Educator Certification, 2013, 7. http://www.michigan.gov/documents/mde/Facts_About_Teacher_Certification_In_Michigan_230612_7.pdf (accessed August 17, 2013).
    In Michigan, for example, the standards for license renewal have been reduced. Prior to 2013, teachers needed to complete eighteen hours in a formal degree program during their first five years of teaching in order to renew their licenses and then six hours every five years after that. Presently, however, they need only complete six hours in a degree program during their first three years and another six hours in the subsequent three years to renew their license a second time. None of the hours need be in the teacher's content area, and the requirements can be alternately met through state-offered equivalency credits. Efforts on the part of state licensing agencies, like Michigan, to deskill the profession only serve to erode the craft.

16. Rosanne Lichatin, interview with Gordon Andrews, September 7, 2011, written responses in Andrews's possession.

17. Nathan McAlister, interview with Gordon Andrews, August 23, 2010, digital tape in Andrews's possession.

18. Darling-Hammond, "Teacher Learning," 93. For an excellent paper framing the issues of teacher knowledge, preparation, and its impact, see *Touch the Future, Transforming the Way Teachers Are Taught: An Action Agenda for College and University Presidents* (Washington, DC: American Council for Education, 1999), 5–26; and John Dewey, *The School and Society* (New York: McClure Phillips & Company, 1900), 19–47.

19. Darling-Hammond, "Teacher Learning," 92.

20. Maureen Festi, acceptance speech at the 2007 Gilder Lehrman History Teacher of the Year Award, New York City. http://vimeo.com/49679324 (accessed April 27, 2015).

21. Examine the following lesson plans by Maureen Festi (5th grade) http://www.eastconn.org/tah/CrossingTheDelaware.pdf (accessed March 20, 2012); Nathan McAllister (middle school) http://centuryofprogress.org/sites/centuryofprogress.org/files/Civil%20War%20Medicine%20Lesson%20Plan%20Summer%202012.pdf (accessed March 20, 2012); and Rosanne Lichatin (high school)

A Craft Approach to Teaching History 57

http://www.gilderlehrman.org/history-by-era/reconstruction/resources/lincoln%E2%80%99s-reconstruction-plan. (accessed March 20, 2012)

22. Segall, "Connection between Curriculum and Instruction," 227.
23. Lichatin, interview.
24. Ibid.
25. Meaghan Glassett, "A Master Teacher," *The Express*, December 3, 2008. http://southshorexpress.com//index.php?option=com_content&view=article&id=2012%3Aa-master-teacher&Itemid=80 (accessed March 10, 2012).
26. Michele Anderson, interview with Gordon Andrews, March 23, 2015, audio tape in Andrews's possession.
27. Pasi Sahlberg, *Finnish Lessons: What Can the World Learn From Educational Reform in Finland?* (New York: Teachers College Press, 2010), 79–80.
28. Peter Stearns, ed., *Benchmarks for Professional Development in Teaching of History as a Discipline*, July 7, 2008. http://www.historians.org/teaching/policy/benchmarks.htm (accessed February 4, 2014).
29. McAlister, interview.
30. Lichatin, interview.
31. McAlister, interview.
32. Ibid.; and Hammond, "Teacher Learning," 91–99.
33. Gordon A. Craig, "History as a Humanistic Discipline," in *Historical Literacy: The Case For History In American Education*, ed. Paul Gagnon and the Bradley Commission on History in the Schools (Boston: Houghton Mifflin Company, 1989), 137.

6 A Collaborative Model for Evaluating Teachers
Why We Need It

Assessment has long been a stress point for history teachers, particularly when they are evaluated by administrators who view history education as a process rather than as a craft. As chapter 5 explained, the collaborative model used by the Gilder Lehrman Institute of American History to determine its national HTOY winner can be adapted for the purposes of developing a teacher evaluation system grounded in authentic disciplinary elements. A defining element of the Gilder Lehrman's assessment of teachers is that the previous year's winner is asked to be a member of the following year's panel. This places them squarely within a paradigm shift that eludes most teachers over their careers. They are directly involved in the assessment of teachers together with a professional historian, a member of the Gilder Lehrman, and Elaine Reed, former executive director of the National Council for History Education. The national winners typically highlight collaboration as essential to their approaches. Indeed, HTOY Roseanne Lichatin's principal approached her to participate in the evaluation process at her high school.[1]

Using the HTOY model, this chapter examines how evaluation of good history teaching can account for the disciplinary elements. The collaborative model explained in this chapter stands in stark contrast to the checklist assessments used commonly from large urban areas to small rural districts.[2] The parameters of the collaboration include teachers, unions, administrators, and a prescribed use of professional learning communities (PLCs) within the discipline of history. At the center of the current evaluation crisis explored here is the misapplied use of "best practices" coupled with policies of the No Child Left Behind (NCLB) and the Race to the Top initiative. Compared to the collaborative model explained here, these policies ignore research on historical thinking, testing, and teacher evaluation to the detriment of effective history education.

THE PROBLEM WITH "PLAYING SCHOOL" AND EVALUATION

A disconcerting dichotomy exists between the way teachers are evaluated using established best practices in the history classroom and what current research demonstrates regarding the use of historical thinking as a

A Collaborative Model for Assessing Teachers 59

pedagogical construct. The problem is due largely to the epistemological underpinnings of best practices, which emerged from education practitioners who relied heavily on the cognitive sciences. Unfortunately, the best practices studies offered as generalizable applications across fields of study disregarded particular disciplinary requirements.[3] The argument here is that best practices literature creates an unnecessary division between the way content pedagogy should be delivered and the way it is evaluated in the classroom. The evaluation problem is comparable to the way canned curricula are used in classrooms to mimic historical thinking but never actually take students into content rich and historically authentic experiences. An evaluation process that avoids historical thinking in the classroom leads participants into "playing school." Lessons have the appearance of historically educative value but none of the substance.

Historical thinking confronts and analyzes what it means to teach and learn in a historically relevant and authentic way. This undertaking has significant consequences for every area critical to the teaching of history. Sam Wineburg argues that the study of history does not merely consider the sorts of content knowledge that *may* lead citizens to think in a civically responsible fashion or to debate which content is more worthy than another. His position "is that history holds the potential, only partly realized, of humanizing us in ways offered by few other areas on the school curriculum," and indeed, when examined properly, that history helps us to uncover the "other," which moves us closer to understanding humanity.[4] Accepting this premise, the implications for teaching students, evaluating teachers, and conducting meaningful research, will require substantive changes in the current evaluation models. Many of those models require cumbersome lists of teacher activities that require administrators to monitor over seventy assessed categories in a fifty-minute lesson.[5]

Whether one is discussing whole group instruction, cooperative learning, inquiry-based models, or the use of technology in the classroom, all popular instructional models, there are few studies that address the disconnect that exists between literature that requires or insists upon the implementation of best practices, and the burgeoning literature in the field that demonstrates the efficacy of implementing historical thinking in the classroom. Since the early 1990s, studies focusing on historical thinking have gained momentum among academics and history educators. For instance, Sam Wineburg's *Historical Thinking and Other Unnatural Acts*, the National Research Council's *How Students Learn History in the Classroom*, along with the more recent works of scholars such as Laura Westhoff, Bruce VanSledright, Peter Seixas, and Linda Levstik all examine the teaching of history as a discipline.[6]

The use of best practices in schools has been considered the gold standard providing epistemological underpinnings for what constitutes good teacher education, professional development, and assessment of teachers in the field. The question of what defines best practices has been aptly addressed

60 *Argument for the Space to Think and Teach*

by Gayle Gregory and Terence Parry in their book *Designing Brain-Compatible Learning*.

> By applying what is known about how the brain learns to classroom practice, pedagogical researchers and other educational professionals have identified a number of powerful instructional techniques that enhance learning, can be generalized across all areas of the curriculum, and can be applied at all grade levels. These are sometimes referred to as "best practices," which means that they have a sound research base and a proven track record in the classroom.[7]

Before examining the virtues of the historical thinking practices infused in HTOY model of teacher evaluation, it is necessary to compare how best practices and historical thinking define inquiry strategies.[8]

COMPARING "BEST PRACTICES" AND HISTORICAL THINKING ON INQUIRY

Best practices' use of inquiry as a methodology is intended to get learners into the habit of using their critical thinking skills, as well as developing research, writing, and presentation abilities. The types of inquiry advocated in the literature encourage individual research, group research, and case studies, and also allow students free rein in the selection of a research topic. On the whole, the inquiry method is closest to matching the literature on historical thinking, but again it veers toward the social studies format, locked in a constructivist paradigm.[9] Real historical inquiry is more complicated and nuanced, requiring a deft understanding of the secondary and primary sources that could provide a substantive explanation for how we have arrived at our current circumstances. So, whereas inquiry is used as a way to stimulate and pique an interest in students toward uncovering the past, its constructivist paradigm precludes students from obtaining real historical understanding.

In *Universal Teaching Strategies*, Amy Driscoll and Jerome Freiberg address the topic of student interest under the heading "Reflective Teaching and Learning: Students as Shareholders." Best practices literature advocates this method because "they may discover how to solve problems, answer questions, draw conclusions, and take responsibility for their own learning. These strategies reflect a philosophy of education that views the learner as a source of knowledge rather than a blank slate upon which the teacher inscribes information."[10] As students take responsibility, they become invested in real inquiry, developing ownership in learning, which in turn leads to advanced levels of critical thinking. Holt and Kysilka have also weighed in on the subject of inquiry, advocating that students be allowed to follow their own interests, in keeping with the philosophy of Carl Rogers.[11]

A Collaborative Model for Assessing Teachers 61

However, none of these authors address how this might translate into good historical research. Instead we are left to conclude that the heightened interest level will inevitably lead to the kind of critical thinking that produces historical understanding.

In contrast to the best practices' advice on inquiry, the use of historical thinking as a pedagogy mirrors the way historians pursue their craft. The state of California, for instance, acknowledges the importance of disciplinary elements of history since its state standards specifically address historical thinking.[12] The pending C3 Michigan curriculum also recognizes historical thinking in its draft standards.[13] Sam Wineburg, in *Historical Thinking and Other Unnatural Acts*, addresses how to think historically with its focus on students, teachers in training, professors, and teachers with various degrees of experience. Wineburg's research reveals that the key to teaching history is the transference of knowledge from professional to student and that it requires special training to accurately approach topics with a professional historian's eye toward the cultural, social, and political realities of that period.[14] And just as teachers need to be specially trained, so too do those in charge of evaluating history teachers in the classroom. This research is also borne out in studies published by the National Research Council in *How Students Learn History in the Classroom*, in which teachers and students actively demonstrated the importance of historical approaches in separating historical events from historical accounts to address the nuances of history.[15]

Best practices literature on inquiry also neglects the counterintuitive nature of real historical inquiry. In "Understanding History," Peter Lee explains that historical learning occurs on two distinct levels. Level one involves all of the areas that we would normally ascribe to content knowledge, whereas level two is where substantive learning occurs. Level two incorporates many of the notions touched upon by Wineburg. However, Lee takes the importance of teaching even further, commenting on the significance of historically trained teachers in the classroom.[16] To those who conduct research on historical thinking, disciplinary knowledge is important because it is the conduit through which teacher practitioners can learn the tools of the trade. Just as assessment drives curriculum and how it is taught in the classroom, so too does the evaluation of teachers drive their pedagogical approaches and ability to teach authentic history.

Comparing best practices and historical thinking on inquiry, it is clear that the two fields of research seldom engage each other. One explanation might be that among the researchers of best practices, the dominant epistemology accepts as sacrosanct the constructivist paradigm and the current brain research, which pulls those researchers in the direction of a social studies mode of instruction. Social studies is also a Progressive Era innovation that focuses less on the discipline of history and more on engaging students in solving current societal issues rather than engaging history on its own terms. The social studies have always emphasized citizenship and character development, as well as the creation of an engaged citizenry that wants

62 *Argument for the Space to Think and Teach*

to improve society by drawing upon relevant historical examples as a way to solve current societal ills. As the child of John Dewey's constructivism and progressivism, this connection between best practices and social studies makes sense. Future research should examine if the best practices can be combined in a fashion that provides a functional pedagogy for historical instruction, or whether they should be confined to other fields of inquiry. Until that research occurs, however, the unfortunate reality is that history teachers on a routine basis are confronted with evaluation systems that ignore the disciplinary features of historical study and instead, assess teachers based on best practices.[17]

When discussing the difference between the period before NCLB and the period that followed, HTOY winner Nathan McAllister thought deeply for a moment and then replied that the real difference was "trust." He said, "You can frame it any way you would like, but before No Child Left Behind, there was more trust and respect between teachers and administrators. We trusted one another. That [trust] has disappeared and we need to reestablish that relationship." When asked to explain by way of example, Nathan was quick to point out that in one of the formative periods of his career as a young untenured teacher, he had a principal who approached teaching as a craft. Nathan extolled the virtues of his principal, who had two doctorates, and described the relationship he had with teachers and teaching. He related how his principal conducted evaluations. When they talked about teaching before, during, and after evaluations, the principal not only talked about Nathan's classroom performance but also about the nature of teaching and how to push forward, always aiming to improve as a craft. This is the type of conversation among principals and teachers that is missing in the post-NCLB era.[18]

NCLB AND THE USE AND ABUSE OF TESTING

In 2001 NCLB was ushered in with bi-partisan fanfare, promising reform with accountability that would result in all children becoming proficient in reading and math by 2014. Among other problems, the legislation ignored the history of global educational reform movements. In S. G. Grant's *History Lessons*, for example, he noted that "in sixty years of vast international research on school testing, the policy of emphasizing test performance in order to improve education has never been validated." Grant then added that "in the 10 years since this accusation, the scene is hardly any clearer."[19]

Despite its many flaws, NCLB became the law of the land with profound implications for public schools. In *The Death and Life of the Great American School System: How Testing and Choice are Undermining Education*, Diane Ravitch exposed its flaws. Schools were required to develop testing regimes for students in grades three through eight, and high school, leading

A Collaborative Model for Assessing Teachers   63

to 100 percent student proficiency by 2014. To bolster accountability there were penalties for schools not meeting NCLB standards. They included everything from providing tutoring, transporting students to another school, to ultimately "restructuring." Restructuring included a range of options from turning the school over to a charter, to the more vaguely outlined ". . . major restructuring of the school's governance."[20]

What this new testing regime did was to not only foster the exponential growth of the testing industry, and costs to schools, but also the spurious propagation of assertions that tougher teacher evaluation would elevate student outcomes. So as 2014 approached, and the reality that 100 percent of America's students were not going to obtain proficiency, waivers from the Obama administration's Department of Education were issued to states that agreed to a new set of expectations. "In 2012, the Obama administration began offering flexibility to states regarding specific requirements of NCLB in exchange for rigorous and comprehensive state-developed plans designed to close achievement gaps, increase equity, improve the quality of instruction, and increase outcomes for all students. Thus far 42 states, DC and Puerto Rico have received flexibility from NCLB."[21]

The Obama administration rolled out its plan, Race to the Top, which dangled four hundred million dollars to be divided among those states fortunate enough to be selected. This happened, of course, only after states had developed new testing and teacher evaluation schemes that used "value-added measurement" (VAM) to demonstrate student growth and teacher accountability. Problematically, the VAMs applied to schools operated on two faulty notions. The first is that teachers are the single most important factor in the education of child. The second is that high-stakes standardized tests are an accurate measure of learning. Experts in the field of evaluation like Linda Darling-Hammond, Ann Lieberman, David C. Berliner, and Gene V. Glass have warned against the use of value-added measurements, exactly because of their inability to measure the impact of teachers on student learning with any validity.[22] As Berliner has argued, NCLB holds that "teachers are the most significant influence in a child's education," and yet nothing could be further from the truth.[23] Teachers are essential to a quality education. However, it is also true that there are myriad influences beyond a teacher's control that significantly impact a student's performance in school. The American Statistical Association in 2014 argued with great precision why VAMs should not be used to measure teacher effectiveness when it stated that:

> Research on VAMs has been fairly consistent that aspects of educational effectiveness that are measureable and within teacher control represent a small part of the total variation in student test scores or growth; most estimates in the literature attribute between 1% and 14% of the total variability to teachers. This is not saying that *teachers* have little effect on students, but that variation among teachers accounts for a small part

of the variation in scores. The majority of the variation in test scores is attributable to factors outside of the teacher's control such as student and family background, *poverty* [italics added], curriculum and unmeasured influences.[24]

Compounding the problem of teacher evaluation is that these VAMs now make up 50 percent of teachers' evaluations in many states like Michigan.[25] The impact on classroom history teachers is evident and detracts from what master teachers try to accomplish in their classrooms. Michele Anderson, the 2014 HTOY, observed that she spends too much time performing pre-tests on her students when she understands what they need and how she wants to design units.[26] Instead, she is required to take time from teaching to perform these pre-tests to accommodate a flawed practice, disguised as best practices.[27] In most districts, then, the other half of teacher evaluation consists of an evaluation device like the popular Danielson Model. This model, used by half of the nation's schools, has more than seventy different measures to be taken by an administrator during a class period.[28] This, of course, has become increasingly difficult, so some states, like Michigan, have legislated that a classroom observation does not have to be for an entire class period.[29] The effect on the profession generally, and the teaching of history in particular, has further eroded the craft of teaching.

One of the main reasons for the erosion of trust that Nathan McAlister indicated is that the regime ushered in by NCLB was, in Ravitch's words, meant to "measure and punish."[30] Unfortunately these current reforms are reactionary and are more reminiscent of the profession one hundred years ago, rather than building for the future. Larry Cuban has written about the shortcomings of evaluation during the 1920s that are eerily present today. For example, Cuban related the findings of Albert Hartwell, the Buffalo superintendent who found that many principals and supervisors inspired fear, and finalized evaluations after observing fragments of a class rather than observing an entire period. Too often teachers feel much the same dread today.[31]

Not all systems ignore good practices in teacher evaluation. States like Connecticut, for instance, are using collaborative models based on model standards.[32] HTOY Rosanne Lichatin's West Morris Regional High School District in New Jersey also relies on content experts for teacher evaluation. She has been serving in an administrative capacity evaluating social studies teachers in the field in collaboration with administrators and teachers. She relayed, for example, how in her district if a teacher was evaluated four times during the year, it would not be uncommon for her to perform three of the four observations.[33] Such examples are unfortunately exceptions to the types of evaluation regimens that most history teachers are forced to endure. What follows is an exploration of a possible evaluation model using the HTOY Rubric with some slight modifications.

VISIONS OF THE POSSIBLE: HTOY TEACHER EVALUATION RUBRIC

"Professions generally set and enforce standards in three ways: (1) through professional accreditation of preparation programs; (2) through state licensing, which grants permission to practice; and (3) through advanced certification, which is a professional recognition of high levels of competence."[34] It is unfortunate that teaching is one of the only professions that does not demand such high standards. There are a number of states that have undermined teacher certification through "alternative" measures that actively undermine the teaching profession such as Teach for America, or state programs available in New York or Texas, for example. It is quite clear that in many states and districts, master teachers are absent from effective collaboration that could enrich and revitalize the profession.

A fundamental strength of the HTOY model is that it is collaborative, involving vital roles for unions, administrators, teachers, and PLCs. It also has the advantage of unlocking the human capital that already exists in every district, but is underutilized, if not ignored. This means there is little to no extra cost to districts and follows many of the high standards set by the National Board for Professional Teaching Standards. There is also the added benefit of disciplinary specificity that allows teachers to be evaluated for teaching content-rich, historically authentic lessons.

The HTOY process outlined below could be easily accommodated by teachers, unions, and administrators as they negotiate these parameters routinely. For background material, teachers are required to supply the following:

- A current resume/curriculum vitae
- A statement of the nominee's philosophy of teaching and how it relates specifically to his or her instruction of American history (one page)
- A sample lesson plan that can be completed in one to two class sessions, demonstrating the use of primary sources (up to five pages)
- A sample extended student project, demonstrating the use of primary documents, artifacts, historic sites, oral histories, and other primary resources (up to fifteen pages)

This material requires history teachers to reflect on their craft and what they have accomplished over a defined period of time. Keeping one's curriculum vitae up to date is viewed as superfluous in most districts. However, this simple practice provides ample evidence of professional pursuits and opens opportunities for teachers to reflect on the trajectory of their career. It also provides answers to basic questions evaluators would ask regarding a professional disposition. For example, what organizations have you joined? What graduate classes have you taken? Do those classes apply to history?

66 *Argument for the Space to Think and Teach*

Have you written and submitted articles? Have you attended history conferences, seminars, or workshops in your chosen field? Have you undertaken the preparation of a book? An up-to-date curriculum vitae demonstrates for the teacher, school, district, and state, a level of intellectual curiosity, accountability, and purpose to a career.

Additionally, the sample lesson, unit, and philosophy required are simply the evidence of a teacher who is thoughtfully pursuing ever-effective ways of teaching. What professional does not evolve in these critical areas? The material also forms the basis of substantive discussion that invigorates PLCs. Think of the opportunities that would present themselves for a department to gather together, tenured, non-tenured, and master teachers, together discussing these key issues in a format that allows for continuous organizational and departmental renewal. The rubric provides concrete agenda items for an intellectually vibrant history community as individuals make their way through a career. No master craftsman is the same after thirty years, nor should any teacher feel comfortable asserting he or she is. Conversations like those outlined here demand that teachers think deeply, be creative, and contribute to the betterment of the whole. These requirements also form the basis of a collaborative model for evaluation that focuses the entire school. Importantly, it creates an opening for content specialists, administrators, and teachers to collaborate during the evaluation. From the very beginning then, there are meaningful conversations about what occurs in the classroom before a classroom observation.

Once in the classroom the collaboration continues between the evaluator(s) (content specialist/administrator) as they discuss the teacher's approach to the lesson. In this case the rubric directly addresses American history but could easily be adapted for any type of history class. It also has the distinct advantage of having three areas of evaluation rather than the seventy or more areas employed in more than half the districts in the United States.[35] An added advantage is that the first category is completed before the evaluator enters the room. Once a teacher satisfies a majority of the criteria in a group, that teacher is qualified in that group. For instance, if an evaluator concluded that a teacher satisfied three of the four criteria in the "excellent" category, and one in the "good" category, that teacher would qualify as "excellent" in his or her commitment to teaching American history. It would also provide ample opportunity to discuss how a teacher could move up to receiving full marks in the "excellent" category.

I.   Commitment to Teaching American History

Excellent: Excellent reputation as an American history teacher and instructional leader within the school/district

- Regularly participates in, organizes, and/or leads professional development opportunities

A Collaborative Model for Assessing Teachers 67

- Active member or leader in one or more social studies/American history professional organizations
- Very active involvement or leadership in national/state/local historic community, including historical societies, museums, libraries, etc.
- Serves as a school leader in seeking and receiving grants and other opportunities to enhance American history instruction

Good: Strong reputation as an American history teacher within the school/district

- Regularly participates in professional development opportunities
- Member of one or more social studies/American history professional organizations
- Regular involvement or leadership in national/state/local historic community, including historical societies, museums, libraries, etc.
- Actively seeks and receives grants and other opportunities to enhance American history instruction

Sufficient: Good reputation as an American history teacher within the school/district

- Participates in some professional development opportunities
- Member of one social studies/American history professional organization
- Very little involvement or leadership in national/state/local historic community, including historical societies, museums, libraries, etc.

Insufficient: Limited reputation as an American history teacher within the school/district

- Does not participate in professional development opportunities
- Not a member of any social studies/American history professional organizations
- No involvement in national/state/local historic community, including historical societies, museums, libraries, etc.

The protocol for evaluator and teacher would continue with the same criteria. A teacher would be required to satisfy a majority of the requirements in any one category to qualify in that category. The advantage for everyone concerned is that the criteria are consistent and available for all to see. Here again, it provides ample opportunities in the PLCs for teachers, administrators, and evaluators to discuss what each of the areas would look like if fulfilled. The rubric narrows the chance for ambiguity and increases the opportunity for professional and disciplinarily specific conversations. They would explicitly address historical thinking

68　*Argument for the Space to Think and Teach*

and the pedagogical tools needed to enrich the educational opportunities for all students. History, among all the disciplines, is the one uniquely qualified to educate the citizen, and section two allows for many fruitful opportunities to provide content-rich lessons.

II. Creativity and Imagination in the Classroom

Excellent: Lessons/projects demonstrate a wide variety of creative teaching methods (e.g., role play, debate)

- Regularly incorporates activities such as expert speakers, field trips, etc., to enhance American history instruction
- Strongly encourages and incorporates interdisciplinary instruction in teaching American history
- Regularly and effectively encourages students to become globally aware, responsible student-citizens, self-directed learners, and practical problem solvers
- Expertly enhances student literacy skills as historical researchers, critical thinkers, and writers

Good: Lessons/projects demonstrate a variety of creative teaching methods (e.g., role play, debate)

- Periodically incorporates activities such as expert speakers, field trips, etc., to enhance American history instruction
- Regularly incorporates interdisciplinary instruction in teaching American history
- Regularly encourages students to become globally aware, responsible student-citizens, self-directed learners, and practical problem solvers
- Effectively enhances student literacy skills as historical researchers, critical thinkers, and writers

Sufficient: Lessons/projects demonstrate a variety of creative teaching methods (e.g. role play, debate)

- Occasionally incorporates activities such as expert speakers, field trips, etc., to enhance American history instruction
- Sometimes incorporates interdisciplinary instruction in teaching American history
- Shows some encouragement of students to become globally aware, responsible student-citizens, self-directed learners, and practical problem solvers
- Moderately enhances student literacy skills as historical researchers, critical thinkers, and writers

A Collaborative Model for Assessing Teachers 69

Insufficient: Lessons/projects do not demonstrate creativity or variety (e.g. role play, debate)

- Does not incorporate activities such as expert speakers, field trips, etc., to enhance American history instruction
- Does not incorporate interdisciplinary instruction in teaching American history
- Does not encourage students to become globally aware, responsible student-citizens, self-directed learners, and practical problem solvers
- Does not enhance student literacy skills as historical researchers, critical thinkers, and writers

Because section three only has one specification to qualify in a particular category, the evaluator and teacher have a particularly clear understanding of the criteria. It is here that teachers will be able to delve deeply into those elements of the discipline that reveal and challenge so much of what students think they understand regarding history. The argument in this book has been that the pursuit of authentic history instruction and the ability of teachers to be able to effectively use them is critical to the cultivation of historical thinking. It is also a skill that, as Peter Lee has proven, requires deft understanding and professionally trained teachers. This rubric also allows for teachers to continually develop and contribute to their own careers, as well as the intellectual and civic communities in which they are vitally connected.

III. Effective use of primary sources

Excellent: Regularly and effectively uses a wide range of primary sources in class and student assignments
Good: Periodically uses primary sources in class and student assignments
Sufficient: Occasionally uses primary source documents in class and student assignments
Insufficient: Does not use primary source documents in class and student assignments

The absence of collaboration addressed in the beginning of this proposal is partly responsible for the current top-down trends in teaching. Resulting too often in teach-to-the-test formats, teachers are trained to deliver synchronized lessons that rob them of their creativity. For any profound change to occur, there must be a paradigmatic shift away from the current adherence to the global educational reform movement model begun in the 1980s.[36] That model is based on a neo-liberal ideology that venerates free-market solutions that have largely resulted in the denigration of teaching in particular and public schools in general. Instead, we need to move toward a model of collaboration that honors the teaching of history as a craft. This book offers working models and reasonable suggestions that can be replicated at little or no fiduciary

70   *Argument for the Space to Think and Teach*

obligation. It does so by demonstrating how to connect the vital interests of already existing institutions, teachers, and administrators with in our universities and public schools. Importantly, this chapter illustrates how these groups are already intertwined as vested groups in a dynamic mission that understands the importance of professional and craft-oriented collaboration.

NOTES

1. Rosanne Lichatin, interview with Gordon Andrews, March 23, 2015, digital tape in Andrew's possession.
2. New York City Department of Education. http://schools.nyc.gov/AboutUs/default.htm (accessed May 28, 2014).
3. See, for instance, Sam Wineburg, "Beyond 'Breadth and Depth': Subject Matter Knowledge and Assessment," *Theory into Practice* 36:4(1997), 255–61.
4. Sam Wineburg, *Historical Thinking and Other Unnatural Acts: Charting the Future of Teaching the Past* (Philadelphia: Temple University Press, 2001), 5.
5. See, for example, Danielson Model: Charlotte Danielson, *The Framework for Teaching Evaluation Framework* http://www.google.com/?gws_rd=ssl#q=charlotte+danielson+model+of+teacher+evaluation (accessed April 24, 2015).
6. Susanna M. Donovan and John D. Bransford, *How Students Learning History in the Classroom* (Washington, DC: The National Academies Press, 2005). Other works on historical thinking have been identified in other chapters. The point here is that whereas the literature on historical thinking is already vast, it has not been acknowledged in the field of teacher evaluation. Whereas the Danielson model acknowledges the importance of disciplinary knowledge, it does not use it beyond the novice level of application.
7. Gayle Gregory and Terence Parry, *Designing Brain-Compatible Learning* (Thousand Oaks, CA: Corwin Press, 2006), 34.
8. Larry C. Holt and Marcella L. Kysilka, *Instructional Patterns: Strategies for Maximizing Student Learning* (Thousand Oaks, CA: SAGE Publications, 2006), 135–39.
9. Steven Zemelman, Harvey Daniels and Arthur Hyde, *Best Practice: New Standards for Teaching and Learning in America's Schools* (Portsmouth, NH: Heinemann Press, 1998), 139–43.
10. Freiberg and Driscoll, *Universal Teaching Strategies,* 305.
11. Holt and Kysilka, *Instructional Patterns,* 207.
12. Framework for the California State Standards http://www.cde.ca.gov/ci/hs/cf/hssfwforfieldreview.asp (accessed April 27, 2015).
13. Although still pending Michigan legislative approval, financing for their adoption is a likely indicator of legislative good will.
14. Wineburg, *Historical Thinking and Other Unnatural Acts,* 63–86.
15. Donovan and Bransford, *How Students Learn History in the Classroom,* 179–209. Also see Bruce A. VanSledright, *Assessing Historical Thinking & Understanding: Innovative Designs for New Standards* (New York: Routledge, 2014).
16. Peter Lee, "Putting Principles into Practice: Understanding History," in *How Students Learning History in the Classroom,* 75–86.
17. On the disciplinary dynamics and history of social studies, see, for instance, Kieren Egan, *Getting it Wrong from the Beginning: Our Progressivist Inheritance from Herbert Spencer, John Dewey, and Jean Piaget* (New Haven: Yale University Press, 2002); and Ronald W. Evans, *The Social Studies Wars: What Should We Teach the Children?* (New York: Teachers College Press, 2004).
18. Nathan McAllister, interview with Gordon Andrews, April 6, 2015, digital tape in Andrews' possession.

A Collaborative Model for Assessing Teachers 71

19. S.G. Grant, *History Lessons: Teaching, Learning, and Testing in U.S. High School Classrooms* (Mahwah, NJ: Lawrence Erlbaum Associates, Inc., Publishers, 2003), 129–30.
20. Diane Ravitch, *Death and Life of the Great American School System: How Testing and Choice Are Undermining Education* (New York: Perseus Books Group, 2010), 97–99.
21. U.S. Department of Education, http://www.ed.gov/esea (accessed April 24, 2015).
22. For an excellent examination of value-added models and their inability to render reliable and valid results, see Linda Darling-Hammond and Ann Lieberman, ed., *Teacher Education around the World: Changing Policies and Practices* (New York: Routledge, 2011); and David C. Berliner, Gene V. Glass, and Associates, *50 Myths & Lies that Threaten America's Public Schools: The Real Crisis in Education* (New York: Teachers College Press, 2014), 50–56.
23. Berliner and Glass, *50 Myths and Lies*, 50–51.
24. American Statistical Association, *ASA Statement on Using Value-Added Models for Educational Assessment, Executive Summary*, April 8, 2014.
25. Ibid.
26. Michele Anderson, interview with Gordon Andrews, March 23, 2015, digital tape in Andrews's possession.
27. Michigan Legislature, *The Revised School Code (Excerpt) Act 451 of 1976*, 380.1249: Performance evaluation system for teachers and school administrators; requirements; recommendations; compliance with subsection (2) or (3) not required; effect of collective bargaining agreement. Sec. 1249. 2(a) (i), http://www.legislature.mi.gov/(S(rpqgl35shsjaedbgqamqqxor))/mileg.aspx?pa ge=GetObject&objectname=mcl-380–1249 (accessed April 24, 2015).
28. Danielson, *The Framework for Teaching Evaluation Framework*.
29. Michigan Legislature, *The Revised School Code (Excerpt) Act 451 of 1976*, 380.1249, 2 (c) (iii).
30. Ravitch, *Life and Death of the Great American School System*, 93.
31. Larry Cuban, *How Teachers Taught: Constancy and Change in American Classrooms 1880–1990* (New York: Teachers College Press, 1993), 59–61; and Valarie Strauss, "US Teachers Job Satisfaction Craters—Report," *The Washington Post*, February 21, 2013. http://www.washingtonpost.com/blogs/ answer-sheet/wp/2013/02/21/u-s-teachers-job-satisfaction-craters-report/ (accessed April 25, 2015). American teachers' job satisfaction is at a twenty-five-year low, with only 39 percent of teachers reporting that they "very satisfied" according to the 29th Annual Met Life Survey of the American Teacher.
32. Linda Darling-Hammond, *Getting Teacher Evaluation Right: What Really Matters for Effectiveness and Improvement* (New York: Teachers College Press, 2013), 117–19.
33. Lichatin, interview.
34. Linda Darling-Hammond, "Teacher Preparation and Development in the United States: A Changing Policy Landscape," in *Teacher Education around the World*, 142.
35. Danielson, *The Framework for Teaching Evaluation Instrument* http://www. google.com/?gws_rd=ssl#q=charlotte+danielson+model+of+teacher+evaluat ion (accessed April 24, 2015).
36. Pasi Sahlberg, *Finnish Lessons: What Can the World Learn from Educational Change in Finland* (New York: Teachers College Press, 2011), 99–100.

Part III

Collaborating to Create Authentic Historical Thinking and Learning

Meaningful, long-term collaboration requires more than just proximity or familiarity. Personal relationships between area high school and university instructors may make the first stages of a project agreeable but cannot guarantee success. Progress, in designing models of co-or complementary instruction, comes only with sacrifice and a shared commitment to incremental improvement. True collaboration works when participants unite behind a common vision, agree to test unproven methods, and respond to unanticipated challenges. Chapters in this section weigh the advantages and challenges of a collaborative approach to the teaching of historiography.

Over the past decade, faculty from WMU, GVSU, and three Kalamazoo-area high schools have worked to integrate elements of historiography into traditional and nontraditional high school curriculum. The following considers the practical benefits of historiography in these environments. Individual chapters highlight theories of instruction and put theory to practice through classroom narratives. A variety of grade and ability levels are considered. Separate collaborative efforts among PCHS, a public school located in suburban Kalamazoo, and several regional alternative high schools provide a diversity of experiences and outcomes.

7 Historiography in the High School Classroom
A Review of the Literature

Over the past decade, history education scholars have written increasingly about how the incorporation of historiography in high school classes might both elevate and enliven students' engagement in historical issues. Much of this literature focuses on the ways historiographical understandings might spark students' interest in the underlying structure and purpose of historical investigation. Of course, historiography can be daunting, too, not only for students but also for teachers and even historians. Partly because historiography is so challenging to teach and understand, it is an ideal subject for collaboration among various levels of educators who are concerned with the improvement of younger students' historical knowledge and skills. Before the remaining sections of the book examine how the teaching of historiography impacted history teaching and learning at three area schools, this chapter will examine how scholars have investigated the ways historiographical approaches can be used and communicated by academics, high school teachers, pre-service teachers, and students.

HISTORIOGRAPHY AND HISTORY EDUCATION DURING SOCIAL STUDIES' HEYDAY

History education specialists started to write about the importance of historiography in teaching secondary-level history beginning in the 1960s. Before that decade, during the subject's first half-century, social studies education specialists generally dismissed the importance of historiography. This avoidance of historiographical investigations has much to do with the origins of social studies education. Beginning with the landmark 1916 NEA *Report on Social Studies*, leading advocates of a more contemporary orientation for historical study in the schools, especially James Harvey Robinson, argued that history for history's sake, with which historiography was associated, had little utility in the schools. In his most important book, *The New History: Essays Illustrating the Modern Historical Outlook*, Robinson included a detailed examination of the evolution of historical writing, from works meant to inspire "primitive literary, political, military, moral,

76 Creating Historical Thinking and Learning

and theological" interests to attempts to apply more scientific principles of investigation. However, Robinson believed that use of more scientific methods would encourage more interest "in explaining the immediate present, and fortunately his sources for the last two or three centuries are infinitely more abundant and satisfactory than for the whole earlier history of the world." Especially promising for Robinson about the new historical methodologies and emphases, due partly to its new alliances with other social sciences and particularly focused on topics other than political and intellectual history, was its relevance for industrial education. "To me it seems obvious that just the sort of facts that we have been reviewing are precisely those which we should be particularly anxious that the boys and girls in the industrial school should be aware of and should lay to heart . . ." Ultimately, for Robinson, the focus of historical instruction should be "to cultivate a progressive spirit in our boys and girls. They are not made to realize the responsibility that rests upon them—the exhilaration that comes from ever looking and pressing forward."[1]

Particularly during the 1930s to 1960s heyday of social studies, historiography held little appeal. For instance, in Edgar B. Wesley and Stanley P. Wronski's *Teaching Social Studies in High Schools*, first published in 1937, the authors devote only one of thirty-seven chapters to history. (Interestingly, the title of that chapter is "Teaching about the Past." The authors avoid using the term *history*.) In that chapter, they allocate space to historical criticism, including issues like the purpose and value of different types of sources, but they say nothing about historiography. Indeed, they downplay the importance of history relative to the social sciences because the latter delve into current issues—the focus of social studies instruction. As Wesley and Wronski say, "Perhaps the most productive functional use to which the study of history can be put is to enlarge and refine the students' understanding of basic social, economic, and political concepts." That is, its value does not depend on anything intrinsic to the discipline; its value is largely supportive of other social sciences.[2]

Maurice P. Hunt and Lawrence E. Metcalf's *Teaching High School Social Studies: Problems in Reflective Thinking and Social Understanding*, first published in 1955, was one of the most influential textbooks on the subject of social studies teaching during the subject's heyday. Their text includes one chapter (out of nineteen) on the subject of history teaching, and it is generally dismissive of the subject. "Despite the amount of instructional time devoted to history there is general dissatisfaction with the results." They claim that historians typically do not use a scientific approach, like other social sciences, with the result that "the dominant approach in secondary school largely promotes the learning of arbitrary associations, and generalizations cast in the past-tense rather than the present." Because historians largely refuse to apply their findings to the present, they say it "is doubtful that students can remember and use historical data." Hunt and Metcalf go on to say that the best use of history is as a kind of "springboard."

Historiography in High School Classrooms 77

"High-school students who study history can increase their understanding of the present only to the extent to which they can be led to hypothesize about the present meaning of past events." By "springboard" they mean that historical data can be transformed into hypotheses that can be tested and turned into problem-solving discussions. The value of historical study for its own sake is completely ignored.[3]

Launching of Project Social Studies through the Division of Educational Research in the U.S. Office of Education in 1962 attempted to reinvigorate social studies education. Now known as the "new" social studies, a number of projects, including curriculum centers and materials, research projects, and textbooks, devoted to social issues inquiry were promulgated. Most of them stressed the inadequacy of historical teaching and methods. Byron G. Massialas and C. Benjamin Cox's *Inquiry in Social Studies*, published in 1966, asserted that "most of the current historiographical problems" in the discipline of history as controversies between historians of the "unique" versus those who pursued the "school of regularities in human conduct." Furthermore, they characterized history's value in the "provision of testable insights and to a lesser extent in the provision of evidential data and case studies" that the more empirically oriented social sciences were better suited to pursue. Donald W. Oliver and James P. Shaver's *Teaching Public Issues in the High School*, also published in 1966, took issue with historians' justification for teaching disciplinary insights simply because they "perpetuate scholarship and 'truth' . . . Such criteria are not adequate for the selection of specific content for the general education high school social studies program."[4]

Near the end of his career, Edgar Bruce Wesley, one of the deans of social studies education, wrote perhaps the most scathing indictment of history education in 1967 in an essay published in *Phi Delta Kappan*. As part of a full-scale attack on the value of history for students, teachers, historians, and the public, Wesley castigated what he described as the historiographical transition from fact-telling to interpretation-telling.

> For generations historians have fretted over the problem of what to write. Should they write the plain unadorned facts or should they select, focus, color, conclude, and recommend? The scientific school led by Stubbs, Maitland, Ranke, and the majority of early American historians tried earnestly to tell the significant facts, believing and hoping that they thus attained truth. Thus the majority of historians for nearly a century tried manfully to be scientific, objective, impersonal, and disinterested. They tried at least feebly to understand and cooperate with the social scientists and to utilize new methods of research and inquiry.
>
> Recently, however, there has been a veritable stampede of historians away from the rigid and exacting standards of the social sciences toward the easy, undefinable, sentimental humanities. This return to the wallows of philosophy, the banalities of the liberal arts, and the

78 *Creating Historical Thinking and Learning*

nebulosities of the humanities will lead, of course, to the lowering of historical standards. Historians will inevitably minimize facts and maximize interpretations. Such soft history will result in soft pedagogy.[5]

Aside from Wesley's inaccurate and arguably, intentionally sarcastic, depiction of historiography, his essay laid down the gauntlet against the value of historiography, ironically, just as social studies itself was fading from the scene. Despite the fact that Project Social Studies inspired a resurgent "new" social studies, it appears in hindsight that the zenith of this movement was reached in the mid-1960s.[6]

To be sure, although the label "social studies" is still used prolifically in the schools and the curriculum, the presentist and problem-solving orientation that characterized the focus of social studies advocates from the 1920s through the 1960s is seldom found in the classroom. It is, however, still found in various texts published for methods instructors. One of the prominent current social studies advocates, Alan J. Singer, devotes a fair amount of attention to history in his *Social Studies for Secondary Schools: Teaching to Learn, Learning to Teach*, which is now in its fourth edition published in 2015. Whereas the term *historiography* is not found in the book, Singer does ruminate on several elements of historiography. For example, he advises future teachers that both facts and interpretations are important: "the facts we consider important are never really separated from the theory we employ or our point of view." He also attempts to reassure future teachers about the lack of scientific truth found in history and historians' reliance on interpretation: "The ultimate check on the historian is the marketplace of ideas where explanations are debated and analyzed, and colleagues are convinced that interpretations explain the data, are logical, are consistent with other things that we know, and provide possibilities for new explanations and further research." Whereas he is certainly more open to the possibilities for historical insights and meanings that his earlier social studies colleagues, Singer nevertheless sees serious problems with how historians formulate their findings. He asks, do historians have "special authority to make moral and political judgments? In this case, not only do I think the answer is no, but I think historians have an obligation to slow the rush to judgment." Here again, as was true of social studies advocates during its heyday years, Singer's advice seems to be to steer clear of the value of historiographical emphases and see history's value more in its provision of facts and data.[7]

HISTORIOGRAPHY AND HISTORY EDUCATION IN THE 1960S AND 1970s

A recognition for the place of historiographical emphases in secondary classrooms in the 1960s and 1970s is probably also linked to the general resurgence of history instruction during that era. Ronald W. Evans, the most

Historiography in High School Classrooms 79

prominent contemporary scholarly advocate for social studies instruction, argues that by the mid-1970s the historical profession, led by the Organization of American Historians (OAH), contended that history teaching had been subsumed into social studies units and multidisciplinary approaches. The OAH and other historical organizations said this situation was no longer tolerable. Whereas Evans attributes historians' concerns to a rising tide of conservatism in the nation as a whole, he also acknowledges that prominent history education scholars such as Kieran Egan criticized social studies instruction as fundamentally flawed because of its primary concern with socializing students instead of introducing them to disciplinary essentials.[8]

With support for social studies instruction dissipating in the 1960s and 1970s, more scholars returned to an emphasis on the value of historical studies. In his 1967 book, *History and the Social Sciences: New Approaches to the Teaching of Social Studies*, Mark M. Krug explains a specific teaching example that illustrates a "new" approach to teaching the American Civil War. Krug's example starts with a teacher writing the names of leading Civil War historians on the board and then adding a summary statement of their views of the causes. According to Krug's example, the teacher would then lead a discussion about the various perspectives. Krug says that presenting divergent views "could make for exciting teaching of Civil War history. It could not only lead to a better understanding of that important period, but would also provide an excellent opportunity for training students in critical and analytical thinking."[9]

In a similar vein, in his 1970 book, coauthored with John B. Poster and William B. Gillies III, titled *The New Social Studies: Analysis of Theory and Materials*, Krug takes social studies advocates like Wesley to task for belittling the value of historical instruction. Contrary to Wesley's claims, Krug says that history instruction should never focus exclusively on facts. Instead, Krug stresses that "History represents the appraisals and reflections upon the past by historians working and writing at a given time. What they write, evaluate, reflect upon, represents as much the date and the circumstances of the historical happening as the date and time when the account is written." In other words, historiography is at the heart of good historical instruction.[10]

C. Benjamin Cox and Byron G. Massialas noted in their *Social Studies in the United States: A Critical Appraisal*, published in 1967, that social studies education had reached a turning point. They directly challenged Krug's perspectives about the need to return to more of a historical grounding in the field of social education. Nevertheless, in asserting the importance of teaching students how to analyze social science data and apply it to contemporary issues—the traditional focus of social studies education—they call on historians to make historiography more explicit in their historical presentations. They take one set of historians to task for moving their discussion of the importance of historiography to the preface where it "might well be passed over by students." Cox and Massialas suggest that if historiography

80 *Creating Historical Thinking and Learning*

was included more systematically in textbooks then students would be better able to apply lessons of the past to their own present-day experiences.[11]

By the 1970s, there seems to have been something of a groundswell to restore the integrity of disciplinary teaching of history in high schools. For example, in a 1971 article titled "History Begins at Home," George McCully argues that history needs to be reintroduced into the high school curriculum, not as a college preparatory course but as a basic course dealing with issues that are fundamental to students' everyday lives. He describes seven elements of well-taught history that provide meaningful perspectives for students: introduction to historical thought; how history affects our lives; autobiography; initial research forays; more in-depth research efforts; and historiography. As pieces of well-taught history courses, each of the seven parts would be engaging and relevant to students in terms of teaching them how complex and therefore, how interesting history is. Historiography is part of the process of reviving intellectual rigor in the schools. Implicit in his article is criticism of social studies curricula as lacking in interest and rigor.[12]

HISTORIOGRAPHY AND HISTORY EDUCATION SINCE THE 1970s

Whereas historiographical instructional emphases can be traced back to the 1960s and 1970s, most of the literature on the value of teaching historiography in high school classrooms has been generated over the past decade. The interest in so-called historical thinking that Sam Wineburg's *Historical Thinking and Other Unnatural Acts: Charting the Future of Teaching the Past* (2001) initiated no doubt contributed to this development. Nevertheless, Wineburg's book and much of the historical thinking literature per se does not delve into the value of educating students about historiography. Part of the reason for this is that much of the historical thinking scholarship is focused on close observation of students' learning behaviors and the way students engage in historical source materials. For instance, Robert Bain notes in his essay, "Into the Breach: Using Research and Theory to Shape History Instruction," that whereas historiography is essential to understanding the structure of the discipline, he advocates teaching students to understand history's disciplinary nature through a more intensive focus, specifically by comparing the differences between history as past occurrence to history as an *account* of past occurrences. Bain's essay provides several examples of activities that help students develop historical thinking skills but not historiography per se.[13]

Moreover, historical thinking, as scholars like Wineburg, Bain, Peter Seixas, and Fritz Fischer have defined it, deals more with the discrete skills or tasks that go into the process of unpacking or uncovering the meaning of historical texts, especially primary source materials. Fischer's list is useful in pinpointing many of these historical skills: raising questions, not providing

Historiography in High School Classrooms 81

definitive answers; using sources; understanding chronology; exploring cause and effect; and examining different points of view and multiple perspectives. Fischer also notes the importance of authorship and crafting arguments but interestingly, does not use the term *historiography*.[14] This may be because, again, historiography strikes even professional historians as challenging and potentially arcane.

Robert P. Green Jr's essay about the use of historiography in high school classrooms focuses on how it can be used to develop students' skills in inductive reasoning. Available historical data and constraints due to perspective always impact historians' conclusions. Therefore, as Green points out, having students analyze the differences among historians' perspectives on a topic develop their critical thinking skills.[15] Engaging in historiography involves all of the significant historical thinking skills but also adds levels of additional complication and effort because it depends on extensive knowledge of a field or fields of history that can only be understood with deep exposure and familiarity. In a recent essay about the value of historiography in teaching high school history, Blake Day highlights the complexity involved in teaching the Cold War's historiography. For instance, he notes the three basic schools of thought on its origins: orthodox, revisionist, and post-revisionist. For students to understand the various schools' perspectives, they need to read enough of the literature involved in each. This is no easy task within the scope of a normal high school unit on the Cold War.[16] Hence, in asking secondary students to develop knowledge of historiography, the problem is how can the deep exposure and familiarity that is normally gained during lengthy scholarly endeavors be overcome?

Laura Westhoff provides one perspective on this question. In an essay focused on what she describes as "historiographic mapping," she says that part of the answer is having students study historiography in the context of a research project. As many historians know, historiography writ large is not only daunting, but it can also be elusive in terms of larger meaning and value. However, as applied to one's own research, the historiography associated with that field is absolutely essential to know. Often only then can one know how one's own research fits into earlier work, and then knowing that helps to frame the way a project's thesis is conveyed.[17]

This aspect of Westhoff's perspective on teaching historiography is very difficult to replicate in a high school classroom. In the PCHS historiography project that subsequent chapters describe, most of the students are enrolled in International Baccalaureate (IB) History classes. The IB History curriculum is tightly defined around fairly focused themes. Students engage in relatively intense study—intense especially as compared to regular history and even Advanced Placement curricula—and are required to write ambitious research papers. But the papers are also tightly scripted in terms of expectations. Those expectations do not lend themselves to the type of historical research papers that Westhoff's historiographical mapping article describes.

82 Creating Historical Thinking and Learning

Westhoff explains that before students can engage in historiography they need to practice and develop the necessary reading abilities. As she says, "Typically, students read both primary and secondary sources for information." They generally do not have the ability to read sources for the "signposts" that contain contextual and/or embedded meanings necessary to decode historical writing. She contends that assignments need to emphasize the "interpretive and argument-driven nature of the discipline." Westhoff also points out that until students practice the historical reading skills necessary for understanding historiography they will not be able to use historiography in their own research process.[18]

Michael Lovorn's recent essay on exposing pre-service teachers to historiography in the methods course tackles another facet of the same problem that Westhoff identifies: How can history teachers make historiography manageable and meaningful? Because historiography is daunting in terms of the time necessary to acquire some understanding of it, he suggests that methods courses focus on historiography in the process of examining local commemorative sites and objects. Examination of material culture artifacts tends to make learning the historiography associated with those items more tangible. This approach has an added benefit of giving pre-service teachers practice in thinking about how to use field trips and commemorative sites in their future secondary classrooms.[19]

Caroline Hoefferle's essay on "Teaching Historiography to High School and Undergraduate Students" tackles another fear of most teachers about the subject: that too much reading focused on theory and philosophy is required of students who study historiography. She notes that careful selection of reading materials can meet this concern head-on: the "amount of reading and the type of reading . . . can be adjusted for any level of history." If students are exposed to historiography, they can then see the "inside story," which also "makes history more alive and interesting to them. It helps them to understand that everything is not already known and agreed upon, that there is a place for them in the profession, [and] that in the future they can contribute to the ongoing historical debates about the past."[20]

In the PCHS historiography project, as Hoefferle suggests in her essays, Andrews, Warren, Cousins, and their pre-service teachers have introduced high school students to the historiography of the Cold War, the Modern Civil Rights Movement, and Mao Zedong's contributions to modern China through concise excerpts of key historians' views. Since this project's origins in 2011, the panel discussions and exercises students engage in then focus on extracting clues about the differences in the historians' perspectives and then articulating how these differences in perspectives matter in terms of the historical issues at hand. The historiographical exposure tends to be fairly intensive but certainly not exhaustive.

David Neumann and David Wrobel's essays provide additional perspectives on the value of teaching historiography to future secondary teachers. Neumann emphasizes how too much history is taught as "disconnected facts" that appears to students as "bulleted lists" instead of as a coherent body of knowledge. The key is finding a way to create this coherence. He suggests that instructors create yearlong courses that emphasize problems in history. He provides an illustration of a course built on the problem of freedom in U.S. history. Students explore the changing meanings of freedom in various periods of the past. The historiography of various periods then informs the way that these changing meanings of freedom are examined.[21] Wrobel's views are similar to Neumann's in terms of the value of problematicizing teaching around key historiographical discussions. The "messy past" that he refers to in his article is messy in part because the historians who have examined any number of issues disagree with each other. Because history does not repeat itself, students need to develop a "historiographical consciousness" that would give them a more sophisticated perspective about various currents of history.[22]

Whereas the literature typically supports incorporation of historiography into the secondary teacher's repertoire, and in this way "close the breach" between teachers and historians, surefire methods of conveying historiography in a way that can become meaningful to teachers in their classrooms are elusive. Barbara Blaszak's essay on introducing historiography to prospective teachers stresses how pre-service teachers typically do not see a connection between historiography and the lessons they want to teach to secondary students.[23] Likewise, Thomas Fallace's essay on historiography and teacher education notes that very often teachers who have been exposed to deeper understandings of the profession still tend to focus on factual presentations with their students. His article explains how he attempted to concentrate on remedying this problem through close attention to production of curriculum in a series of so-called counterpoint history seminars for pre-service teachers. It was not until the third time that he taught the course that he realized that it was crucial to model historiographically informed lessons in the class. Fallace notes that students typically understood a particular field's historiography when they wrote their papers but usually did not modify their curriculum ideas based on historiography until shown how to do this.[24]

Fritz Fischer suggests that one of the best ways to introduce students to historiography is by constructing survey courses around the idea of "uncovering" history. Instead of the relatively passive emphasis on covering history in a chronological narrative fashion, Fischer recommends that teachers base their survey course themes on key historiographical issues. For instance, on the Federal period, he suggests this major historiographical question: How did the role of women change in the late eighteenth and early nineteenth centuries? This question connects directly to a major focus embodied in the historical literature on Republican Motherhood in the period. Using the Grant Wiggins and Jay McTighe *Understanding by Design* unit and lesson planning methodology, this type of question is an "essential" question that helps to frame how units and lessons are developed and implemented. Fischer's suggestion goes a long way toward the goal of incorporating

84 Creating Historical Thinking and Learning

historiography into classrooms in a way that does not necessarily make it a separate focus. Indeed, S. G. Grant and Jill M. Gradwell's *Teaching History with Big Ideas: Cases of Ambitious Teachers* provides specific case studies of how three middle school and five high school history teachers used both big ideas and references to historiography to teach their various topics in a way that they argue makes historical investigations more meaningful for both teachers and students.[25]

Victoria B. Fantozzi describes a collaborative effort between a history graduate student and a social studies education graduate student to co-teach a course for students pursuing master's degrees in social studies education focused on historiographical issues in U.S. history. The social studies education co-teacher took the lead in convincing the students in the class, who were prospective teachers, of the importance of historiography. She claimed most of them did not initially see how it was relevant for their future students. The history co-teacher felt that students should "learn larger historiographical concepts so they could use those concepts in their teaching." Although they co-taught the course, the two instructors never actually worked together during any of the class sessions; they simply alternated teaching the students. Ultimately, Fantozzi concludes that co-teaching is not necessarily the same as collaboration, especially because the social studies education and history perspectives were divergent in many respects. Yet it does seem that even given this divergence in perspectives, both teachers made some gains in helping future teachers see the potential relevance of incorporating historiography into class material.[26]

Carefully crafted and incorporated historiographical emphases in high school classrooms add relevance and meaning to history teachers' repertoire of useful instructional practices. Teachers who carve out room in their curriculum for places where students can engage in historiographical investigations—albeit truncated by time constraints and complexity—are likely to see students' interest in the underlying importance of the subject increase. This is borne out by findings from the PCHS historiography project, which is explored in the following chapters.

NOTES

1. Peter Novick, *That Noble Dream: The "Objectivity Question" and the American Historical Profession* (Cambridge: Cambridge University Press, 1998), 188–89; and James Harvey Robinson, *The New History: Essays Illustrating the Modern Historical Outlook* (New York: The Macmillan Company, 1912). Quoted on pages 39, 68–69, 153, 265.
2. Edgar B. Wesley and Stanley P. Wronski, *Teaching Social Studies in High Schools*, Fifth Ed. (Lexington, MA: D.C. Heath and Company, 1964), 435–57. Quoted on p. 453.
3. Maurice P. Hunt and Lawrence E. Metcalf, *Teaching High School Social Studies: Problems in Reflective Thinking and Social Understanding*, Second Ed. (New York: Harper and Row, Publishers, 1968), 144, 152–54.

Historiography in High School Classrooms 85

4. On the origins of Project Social Studies, see Ronald W. Evans, *The Hope for American School Reform: The Cold War Pursuit of Inquiry Learning in Social Studies* (New York: Palgrave Macmillan, 2011), 89–94; Bryon G. Massialas and C. Benjamin Cox, *Inquiry in Social Studies* (New York: McGraw-Hill Book Company, 1966), 34–36; and Donald W. Oliver and James P. Shaver, *Teaching Public Issues in the High School* (Boston: Houghton Mifflin Company, 1966), 7.

5. Edgar Bruce Wesley, "Let's Abolish History Courses," *Phi Delta Kappan* 49(September 1967), 3–8. Quoted on pp. 6–7.

6. Evans, *The Hope for American School Reform*, 141–49.

7. Alan J. Singer, *Social Studies for Secondary Schools: Teaching to Learn, Learning to Teach*, Fourth Ed. (New York: Routledge, 2015). Quoted on pp. 25, 30, 33.

8. Ronald W. Evans, *The Tragedy of American School Reform: How Curriculum Politics and Entrenched Dilemmas Have Diverted Us from Democracy* (New York: Palgrave Macmillan, 2011), 171–77.

9. Mark M. Krug, *History and the Social Sciences: New Approaches to the Teaching of Social Studies* (Waltham, MA: Blaisdell Publishing Company, 1967), 194.

10. Mark M. Krug, John B. Poster, and William B. Gillies, III. *The New Social Studies: Analysis of Theory and Materials* (Itasca, IL: F. E. Peacock Publishers, Inc., 1970), 168.

11. C. Benjamin Cox and Bryon G. Massialas, eds., *Social Studies in the United States: A Critical Appraisal* (New York: Harcourt, Brace and World, Inc., 1967), 5, 144. Quoted on p. 144.

12. George McCully, "History Begins at Home," *The History Teacher* 4:4(1971), 52–62.

13. Robert B. Bain, "Into the Breach: Using Research and Theory to Shape History Instruction," in *Knowing, Teaching & Learning History: National and International Perspectives*, ed. Peter N. Stearns, Peter Seixas, and Sam Wineburg (New York: New York University Press, 2000), 331–52.

14. Fritz Fischer, "The Historian as Translator: Historical Thinking, the Rosetta Stone of History Education," *Historically Speaking* 12:3(2011), 15–17.

15. Robert P. Green, Jr., "Reconstruction Historiography: A Source of Teaching Ideas," *Social Studies* 82:4(1991), 153–57.

16. Blake Day, "Historiography and the High School Teacher," *Social Studies Review* 52:1(2013), 81–84.

17. Laura M. Westhoff, "Historiographic Mapping: Toward a Signature Pedagogy for the Methods Course," *Journal of American History* 98:4(2012), 1115.

18. Westhoff, "Historiographic Mapping," 1119–25.

19. Michael G. Lovorn, "Historiography in the Methods Course: Training Preservice History Teachers to Evaluate Local Historical Commemorations," *The History Teacher* 45:4(2012), 569–79.

20. Caroline Hoefferle, "Teaching Historiography to High School and Undergraduate Students," *Magazine of History* 21:2(2007), 40–44.

21. David Neumann, "Solving Problems by Creating Problems: Building Coherence in History through Inquiry," *Teaching History* 36:2(2011), 83–96.

22. David M. Wrobel, "Historiography as Pedagogy: Thoughts about the Messy Past and Why We Shouldn't Clean It Up," *Teaching History* 33:1(2008), 3–11.

23. Barbara J. Blaszak, "Preventing 'Back-atcha': Improving Secondary School Instruction by Introducing Prospective Teachers to Historiography," *The History Teacher* 43:3(2010), 435–39.

24. Thomas D. Fallace, "Historiography and Teacher Education: Reflections on an Experimental Course," *The History Teacher* 42:2(2009), 205–22.

86   *Creating Historical Thinking and Learning*

25. Fritz Fischer, "Uncovering History for Future History Teachers," *The History Teacher* 43:3 (2010), 441–48; Grant Wiggins and Jay McTighe, *Understanding by Design*, Expanded Second Ed. (Upper Saddle River, NJ: Pearson Education, Inc., 2006), especially, pp. 105–25; and S. G. Grant and Jill M. Gradwell, eds., *Teaching History with Big Ideas: Cases of Ambitious Teachers* (Lanham, MA: Rowman and Littlefield Education, 2010).

26. Victoria B. Fantozzi, "Divergent Purposes: A Case Study of a History Education Course Co-taught by a Historian and Social Studies Education Expert," *The History Teacher* 45:2(2012), 241–59. Quoted on p. 251.

8 Lifting the Veil
Teachers and Historiography

Over the past two decades, the field of historical thinking has produced a rich and well-accepted body of literature that explores and explains how students learn history. It attempts to make known the "unnatural" aspects of the discipline, revealing the relatively unknown approaches of historians and their craft. The research often focuses on the way in which students engage primary and secondary sources as they construct meaningful historical understandings of change over time. Nevertheless, little attention has been directed to historiography and the vital role it plays in shaping historical thinking. Although their collaborative efforts stretch back over a decade, since 2011 history educators from GVSU and WMU have collaborated with history teachers at PCHS to examine the pedagogical potential of historiography in the classroom. The history educators and teachers have also worked with pre-service teachers, each of whom prepare and conduct lessons incorporating historiography. This chapter explains the varied ways PCHS teachers have employed historiography to develop disciplinary competence and greater interest in the study of history. It is also important to note that whereas the use of historiography enlivens historical pedagogy, it also prepares students for success in college and as citizens.

To many teachers in the field as well as history educators, the introduction of historiography into a classroom as a topic of discussion or as a pedagogical tool is a nonstarter. With everything that a social studies teacher needs to cover in an academic year, who can blame them? Not only is the curricular constriction of a teacher's time a real impediment, but the familiarity of the teacher with the disciplinary knowledge of historiography also acts as a constraint. However, as pointed out about the body of literature reviewed in chapter 7 and has become increasingly evident to the various parties involved in this project since 2011 is that historiography can be a valuable historical pedagogy. Although a Google search reveals that teachers are using historiography to challenge their students, this project is distinctive because it offers a collaborative model that takes advantage of the mutual self-interest of individuals and institutions to understand how historiography can work as an instructional

88 Creating Historical Thinking and Learning

pedagogy. The historiography project at PCHS provides four years' worth of insights into the following questions: How do calls for pedagogical changes in the classroom to use historiography compare to this project's findings? How do teachers in the field introduce historiography to their students? How does the use of historiography add to the disciplinary knowledge of students in a way that contributes to their college readiness and citizenship capabilities?

THE PCHS HISTORIOGRAPHY PROJECT'S ORIGINS

The collaboration with PCHS teachers started as a hopeful conversation regarding a project that would be of mutual interest to everyone involved. In this case it was a conversation on the last days of school as Sara Brown, the PCHS media center's (hereafter library) teacher-librarian, and Gordon Andrews were saying good-bye. Gordon, hereafter noted in first person, had been a history teacher for thirteen years at PCHS before earning his PhD in history at WMU. Sara's background is unique in many ways for a librarian as she came to that role after teaching in the classroom for six years. She has a bachelor's degree in earth science with a minor in math and an MA in education and was teaching math at the time an opening occurred in the library at the high school. She was interested in the position, left the classroom in 2005, and obtained another master's degree in library science from Grand Valley State University. Sara mentioned that there are two basic philosophies about how to manage libraries. One is more passive, where people come to the library and resources are managed, and the other collaborative and entrepreneurial, as librarians seek out partnerships, continually expanding the uses of the library. Sara's philosophy falls into the latter category, and her efforts have been crucial to this study's successes.[1]

That seemingly innocuous conversation about working on a future project soon evolved to include history educators from WMU and GVSU, three PCHS IB history teachers, and Sara. As she reflected on that conversation, Sara recounted that because I was leaving to take a position at GVSU, we simply agreed to "find a way to collaborate that would benefit both levels." That was in the spring of 2009, and in 2010 I reached out to Sara again with a more concrete notion of what the collaboration would look like. We discussed centering the project around historical thinking, "specifically historical comprehension, analysis and interpretations," as she recalled. Conversations then evolved to the shape and scope of the collaboration. We discussed teachers who would be interested, broadening the collaboration to include GVSU, WMU, the high school, and the library. At that time we had also decided on the use of historiography in the collaboration. With the parameters of the collaboration established and all parties contacted and agreeing to participate, we held our first meeting in January of 2011.[2]

I had used historiography in my classes at the high school for more than a decade and found students to be genuinely interested in the differing interpretations of historians on the key events we covered. They were not lost or confused by the notion that historians would argue over the meaning of history and found the differing interpretations intriguing. It is also true, as one reads the literature surrounding the use of historiography, that it has long been left to the heady and exclusive terrain of graduate school, steadily working its way down the academic ladder. It has devolved from graduate, to undergraduate, and now has many history educators calling for it use in the high school, as has been pointed out in previous chapters. It made perfect sense, then, that this intriguing area of study be taken from behind the veil and made accessible to secondary students. It requires the same degree of professionalism that teachers ply every day in the classroom. That is, they take tremendously complicated and nuanced material and make it intellectually palatable for the audience they serve. Our first group of teachers was more than prepared for the collaboration and its goals.

PCHS IB HISTORY TEACHERS' BACKGROUNDS

Kent Baker, Sara Brown, Patricia Johnson, and Tama Salisbury are the teachers involved in the historiography project. They embody a range of experiences and academic backgrounds. Patricia Johnson began her forty-three-year career teaching German after graduating from Kalamazoo College, a small liberal arts college with a reputation for preparing good teachers. She later moved into the social studies, teaching American history, Honors American, World History, and IB Twentieth-Century World. Kent Baker graduated from Michigan State University (MSU) with majors in political science and history. After substitute teaching, he enrolled in MSU's post-baccalaureate program and obtained his teacher's license in 2000, when he was hired by Portage Public Schools. Since then he has earned a MA in history that he is able to use frequently in his classroom teaching.[3] Tama Salisbury graduated from MSU in 2005 with a degree in social studies after a yearlong field experience before being hired by PCHS. During her undergraduate preparation, she was purposeful in the selection of extra coursework in political science and history because she wanted to be as prepared as possible for the demands of the classroom. With the extra coursework Tama has earned the same number of credit hours in history that are required in a major. Tama then secured a MA in curriculum and instruction from MSU, including additional coursework in social studies focused on action research.[4] Each teacher agreed in principle to the parameters of the collaboration.

Those parameters included their participation in a pre-assessment and post-assessment with all of their students, including non-IB students.

90 *Creating Historical Thinking and Learning*

The pre-assessment established a baseline of what students understood historiography to be. It also indicated their disposition toward history as a subject of study. The post-assessment evaluated students' knowledge of historiography at the end of the year and measured any increase or decrease in their interest in historiography as a topic and history more generally because of their exposure to historiography. The second obligation involved IB teachers' willingness to work with social studies and history pre-service teachers, who would then present a lesson based on historiography to one or more of their IB classes. They also agreed to be interviewed as part of the study and participate in organizational meetings.

Before becoming an IB school, according to PCHS's principal, Eric Alburtus, the high school had an anemic AP program that in many ways was built to fail. As Eric explained, students had to test to get into honors, and if they fell below a B-, they were removed from the honors program, which fed into the AP classes. Alburtus observed that, "What IB taught us is that kids are a lot smarter than we ever gave them credit for." The district became interested in IB when a teacher whose daughter attended an IB school in California shared the advantages of the curriculum. IB was started in the 1960s as a way to connect American students overseas attending international schools with a unified curriculum. For history courses students read primary sources and monographic literature and are expected to write papers that reflect historical thinking. The district sent a group of teachers, including Eric, who was a classroom teacher at the time, for training, and they came back very impressed.[5]

As he reflected on the differences in curricula, Eric mentioned that before adopting the IB curriculum, PCHS's history teachers never used additional primary or secondary sources with instruction. The history teachers, like those in many high schools, simply used a textbook, so this was a major shift in pedagogy, and Eric added, "let alone the historiographical implications of what IB was trying to do." There was some skepticism on Eric's part regarding the number of students who would volunteer for such a demanding curriculum. He was both a little surprised and very happy to report that around 60 percent of all the students at the high school are currently enrolled in IB courses. "It bounces around," Eric said, "between 57 and 61 percent of our juniors and seniors." Leadership at PCHS is important in creating the space for teachers to challenge students with what makes history fundamentally interesting. Alburtus is not interested in creating an educational aesthetic; rather he and the teachers are interested in cultivating a substantive level of learning.[6]

Because historiography was an integral part of the IB history curriculum, it seemed a natural fit. Nevertheless, the inclusion of historiography in the IB curriculum was not as clear cut as it first seemed. As Blake Day states in, "Historiography and the High School Teacher," AP and IB teachers do address historiography in the classroom. What is left unstated is the fact that the IB curriculum does not explicitly use the term *historiography*.[7] Instead, IB refers to "alternative histories," or "alternative perspectives." Whereas these terms can lead to the use of historiography in the classroom, the terminology adds an unnecessary layer of obfuscation for students who are already unfamiliar with the term. In addition, the term *alternative* is often a reference to fanciful ideas or practices. Nonetheless, because use of historiography is required in students' essays for the IB tests, Pat, Kent, Tama, and Sara were ideal instructors to start the study. The spring of 2015 marked the first year of expanding the study to include a ninth-grade course in non-honors U.S. History.

PCHS IB HISTORY TEACHERS' REFLECTIONS ON HISTORIOGRAPHY'S USE

Based on a recent Delphi panel survey, Bradley Fogo concluded that nine core teaching practices constitute authentic history teaching. His findings also endorse an inquiry-based teaching approach. The nine core practices identified are:

1. Use of Historical Questions
2. Select and Adapt Historical Sources
3. Explain and Connect Historical Content
4. Model and Support Historical Reading Skills
5. Employ Historical Evidence
6. Use of Historical Concepts
7. Facilitate Discussion of Historical Topics
8. Model and Support Historical Writing
9. Assess Student Thinking about History

The results are thought-provoking for a number of reasons. First, the use of historiography as an approach to teaching in the classroom conforms well to the findings of the Delphi survey. All nine teaching practices identified in the survey are part of historiographical investigations. Second, the PCHS teachers exhibit all of the identified core teaching practices in their IB courses. As Fogo's research emphasizes, "Any of the practices identified in this study will be filtered through a teacher's historical and historiographical content knowledge and selected, combined, and pursued in relation to specific groups of students in different learning environments." His research supports the need for teachers to be given the space to think and teach historically.[8]

How do the teachers in question view IB's historiographical requirement, and how do they introduce historiography in the classroom? In a series of interviews conducted in 2014–2015, each teacher participant provided

92 Creating Historical Thinking and Learning

observations on the status of the collaboration. All three classroom teachers welcomed the requirement because of its rigor. Kent Baker stated that the rigorous requirements and use of historiography "stress the need for deep understanding from multiple perspectives." He points out, for example, that students are required to read and discuss multiple sources related to questions surrounding the origins of World War II or the subject of total war.[9] The other teachers echoed the same understanding of how IB addresses historiography by demanding that students address multiple perspectives and also compare and contrast and analyze sources in disciplinarily recognizable ways.[10]

All four teachers involved in the project talk frequently with each other about pedagogy but are comfortable enough to take independent approaches when it comes to introducing historiography into their classrooms. For instance, two of the teachers introduce historiography as the academic year progresses. They found waiting for students to become acclimated to the new course and introducing historiography with research on a unit like the First World War to be effective.[11] Choosing to weave historiography into the fabric of an investigation fits nicely with the suggestion offered by Laura Westhoff in which she points out the pedagogical advantages of using historiography with a research project.[12] Tama, on the other hand, prefers to introduce her students to the topic by taking time at the beginning of the academic year. She uses Conal Furay and Michael J. Salevouris, *The Methods and Skills of History: A Practical Guide*, to help her do this.[13]

In Tama's IB courses, the students spend three to five days examining the nature of history. Tama uses three chapters from the book that address specific elements she feels will help to clarify the discipline for her students. The first chapter, "The Nature of History: History as Reconstruction," where the authors state, for the uninitiated, that "'History,' then, is both the past and the study of the past."[14] Complete with exercises this primer is intended for the collegiate level but can also be used with advanced high school students. After discussion about what history is, Tama has her students take on historiography directly in the "The History of History." The chapter moves from the literal meaning of historiography, "the writing of history," through a survey ranging from Leopold Van Ranke and Karl Marx, to women's history and history in the information age.[15] Although each PCHS IB history instructor uses his or her own approach to the introduction of historiography, each also eschews the notion of "the one right way."

How do the three teachers feel about the use of historiography in the classroom? After all, just because it is a required element of a curriculum does not mean that they find it engaging or particularly useful as a pedagogy. Here the findings were encouraging, as all three teachers found the use of historiography to be helpful in increasing their students' knowledge and interest in history, although as Pat Johnson stated, at times "it's hard

Lifting the Veil 93

to quantify." She went on to observe that students did perform better on the IB writing that year.[16] This, of course, was one of the elements we were interested to learn and were happy to find validated by the data from the post test and student performances on the IB test.[17]

For each IB teacher historiography as a pedagogy is no panacea. As Tama reflected on the results in her classroom, she mentioned that it did improve their basic understanding and improve interest for some, but there were still others who were "unwilling" to embrace the methodology. She went on to explain that for some of her students, who are juniors, it is the first time that they began to understand that history is not just facts. For example, some of her students responded with quizzical expressions when encountering controversy in the texts. Common questions for her to field from her students were "I thought in the text it said x," which then led to questions about sourcing, context, perspective, and authorship. This may be great for the classroom, but you could tell, she said, that it was the first time many students had had to wrestle with historical meaning and importantly, epistemology. Or after reading varied and conflicting inter-pretations on The Long March and Mao's rise to power, some students asked, "So how influential was Mao?" Again, this is exactly the type of questioning we want students to take part in, as they are forced to address history as a discipline and begin to dig deeply into how they understand and formulate their own decisions regarding conflicting historiographical claims.[18]

Kent Baker, whose students are seniors, echoed some of the same senti-ments regarding the effectiveness of historiography as a pedagogical tool. When asked about this, he emphatically stated that there was "no ques-tion that looking at historical perspectives deepens the understanding of history" for his students. For example, after introducing the topic of civil rights, Kent passed out two readings, one from Steven F. Lawson expressing the top-down historiography, and one from Charles Payne articulating his-toriography from the bottom up, that were to be used in the collaboration with the pre-service teachers.[19] Of interest here are the number of questions generated by the students as he passed out the readings. In addition to the usual questions such as, "How much to we have to read?", he also fielded more substantive questions related to what the authors' perspectives might be and how closely should they read the articles. For weeks after the meth-ods students presented their lesson, Kent's students were still bringing up historiographical questions related to the top down, versus the bottom up material from Lawson and Payne. They also were asking how those inter-pretations might apply to other moments in U.S. history. The students were revealing an increased interest in understanding history from a disciplinary perspective.[20]

All three teachers voiced concerns about available time and materials concerning the use of historiography. It does take time to prepare and exe-cute lessons exploring historiography. Whereas the time was a concern for

94 *Creating Historical Thinking and Learning*

the teachers, they also observed how much content gets covered in a discussion that requires students to offer and defend multiple historical perspectives. Additionally these lessons offer profound opportunities for students to render well-thought-out historical judgments. For the first time the veil had been effectively lifted for many of these students on one of the least-taught elements of the craft in high schools across the country.[21]

In response to the pedagogical effectiveness of historiography, the PCHS teachers expressed concerns over how to procure materials for their students. Historians who write for K–12 students need to address this concern. More effective presentation of historiographical materials for younger students could have a profound impact on the craft of teaching history. The question of curricular material also leads to an essential component of our collaboration, and that is the "librarian as teacher." The historian's craft relies on sources, and in the high school a profoundly important resource for those sources is the librarian; at PCHS that job is held by Sara Brown. A tremendously conscientious and energetic person, Sara has been a pivotal element in our collaboration from the beginning. When asked directly if she would be interested in participating with Western Michigan University, Grand Valley State University, history teachers from Portage Central, and methods students from both universities, her answer was short and enthusiastic: "I'm in."[22]

Since that time she has procured books dealing with historiography and helped to organize online panel discussions between GVSU and PCHS students in the media center. Beginning in 2013, Sara was able to convince Portage school administrators to purchase an academic database, JSTOR, which students have taken advantage of by logging in over 1,500 searches and reading over 6,700 pages in some of the most prestigious database holdings of scholarly journals available for historical research. With the availability of the enormous scholarly research database in JSTOR, PCHS teachers can now regularly assign academic research articles to students.[23]

By lifting the veil on historiography, PCHS teachers are able to reveal one of the last remaining elements of the discipline that eludes most students. An introduction to the purposes of historiography does not need to be left to college professors or doctoral students preparing for professional careers in history. High school history teachers, like those participating in this study, are quite capable of introducing students to this part of the discipline. The PCHS IB teachers have shown the ability to engage students' interests in investigating history in a way that shows them how and why historians disagree. In doing so, they lead their students away from the single narrative that plagues the textbooks and stale curricula examined earlier. In point of fact, it leads students into to understand that history is a sanguine discipline worthy of their pursuit.

Collaborations like this one can also aid in narrowing the gap between master teachers and those beginning their careers. Teachers involved in the collaboration have been more than willing to speak with pre-service teachers, before, during, and after their lessons with students. For many of the undergraduates, this is the first time they have been in front of a classroom, and the teachers' feedback has been an important part the pre-service teacher development. For example, all of the GVSU pre-service teachers discussed without prompting the contact they had with the PCHS teachers. The teachers for their part have been candid with the GVSU pre-service teachers about their lesson planning, giving feedback and allowing students to adapt their lesson plans. A frequent observation by the teachers involved has been that they wish they had more contact with the students over lessons. The contact teachers have had with the undergraduates and their own has been demonstrably beneficial to the furthering of historical understanding for all parties involved.

NOTES

1. Sara Brown's personal notes delivered to Gordon Andrews on May 9, 2014. Notes in Andrews's possession.
2. Ibid. For a good description and analysis of collaboration's benefits at the undergraduate level, see Alison Hicks and Adrian Howkins, "Tipping the Iceberg: A Collaborative Librarian-Historian Approach to Redesigning the Undergraduate Research Assignment," *The History Teacher* 48:2(2015), 339–59.
3. Kent Baker, interview with Gordon Andrews, April 23, 2015, audio tape in Andrews's possession.
4. Tama Salisbury, interview with Gordon Andrews, April 23, 2015, audio tape in Andrews's possession.
5. Eric Alburtus, interview with Gordon Andrews, April 23, 2015, audio tape in Andrews's possession. The International Baccalaureate website provides further information on the various programs offered around the globe. See http://www.ibo.org/ (accessed April 20, 2015).
6. Ibid.
7. Blake Day, "Historiography and the High School Classroom," *Social Studies Review* 52:1(2013), 81.
8. Bradley Fogo, "Core Practices for Teaching History: The Results of a Delphi Panel Survey," *Theory & Research in Social Education* 42:2(2014), 151–96.
9. Baker, interview.
10. Pat Johnson, interview with Gordon Andrews, May 9, 2014; and Tama Salisbury, interview with Gordon Andrews, May 9, 2014. Notes in Andrews's possession.
11. Johnson, interview.
12. Laura M. Westhoff, "Historiographic Mapping: Toward a Signature Pedagogy for the Methods Course," *Journal of American History* 98:4(2012), 1114–26.
13. Salisbury, interview; Michael J. Salevouris and Conal Furay, *The Methods and Skills of History: A Practical Guide* (Malden, MA: Wiley Blackwell, 2015).
14. Salevouris and Furay, *The Methods and Skills of History*, 15.
15. Ibid., 255–67.
16. Johnson, interview.
17. PCHS Historiography Project, Post-Assessment Survey, 2014.

96 Creating Historical Thinking and Learning

18. Salisbury, interview.
19. Stephen F. Lawson and Charles M. Payne, eds., *Debating the Civil Rights Movement, 1945–1968* (Lanham, MD: Rowman and Littlefield, 1998).
20. Baker, interview.
21. Baker, Johnson, and Salisbury, interviews.
22. Brown, interview.
23. Ibid.

9 Students and Historiography
How Collaboration Improves Learning

How can we impart the passion, nuance, and complexities of history to secondary school students? Injecting historiographical debates into high school history classes introduces students to the intellectual terrain of the profession, which in turn transforms the subject, usually presented as a static narrative, into its authentic and contested nature. By investigating historiographical debates, students also examine how historians explain change over time. Historiography piques students' intellectual curiosity as they are presented with the real substance of historical inquiry. Reflecting on historiographical debates also helps students understand what it means to be an informed citizen.

This chapter highlights students' involvement in the PCHS historiography project that began in 2011–2012. The collaboration explained in this chapter is grounded in the more than decade-long relationships among the professors and teachers at WMU, GVSU, and PCHS that chapter 4 explained. The collaboration among professors, teachers, and students suggests one path of historical learning reform in schools nationwide. The PCHS project demonstrates how historiography can be infused into historical pedagogy and learning.

When the project was designed, the guiding questions were as follows:

1. Do students understand the role of historiography in the discipline of history?
2. Does an understanding of historiography increase the interest of students in the study of history?
3. Do teachers find the use of historiography an effective pedagogy?
4. Why is it important for secondary students to understand historiography?

To address these questions, Gordon Andrews, Wilson Warren, and James Cousins in collaboration with Tama Salisbury, Patricia Johnson, and Kent Baker selected historiographical readings on the Civil Rights Movement, the Cold War, and the Chinese Communist Revolution. These three historical developments are standard curricular topics, taught nationally as well as in

98 Creating Historical Thinking and Learning

the state of Michigan, although in this case they were taught in the IB History of the Americas and IB Twentieth-Century World courses. The high school teachers presented their students with historiographical readings in preparation for panel discussions. Before the panel discussions, history students were given a pre-assessment, and following the panel discussions, were administered a post-assessment. The pre-assessment and post-assessment consisted of both Likert and short-answer questions. For the purposes of this chapter, the focus is on students who participated in the panel discussions on the historiography of the Civil Rights Movement.

The project's design also featured substantive roles for GVSU and WMU pre-service teachers. The struggle to find substantive field experiences for pre-service teachers is a persistent frustration among history educators. To that end, the professors and teachers extended the project's collaboration to include the pre-service teachers. At both GVSU and WMU, students in senior-year social studies methods courses volunteered to participate in field experiences that required them to create a lesson plan on civil rights, Cold War, or Chinese Communism historiography, and then develop and conduct a panel discussion with the high school students. Because of the distance from Portage Central, the study incorporated technology that allowed GVSU students to Skype into the classroom whereas the WMU students visited the classrooms and conducted their panel discussions in person. Chapter 10 focuses more specific attention on the pre-service teachers.

Although the literature on historiography in high school settings suggests how it can be crucial to improved learning, there have been few attempts to actually study the impact of historiography on high school students' learning, as chapter 7 notes. Revealing the existence of historiographical debates may address a long-standing question on the part of students: What is the purpose of historical study? History educators have long advocated a curriculum that is grounded in disciplinary elements, and clearly one of the essential aspects of historians' profession, as Fritz Fischer points out, is to ask questions.[1] It is therefore important for high school students to know that in pursuing questions involving historical epistemology, historians are not of one mind. By incorporating these historiographical debates into their instruction, teachers can expand their curricular repertoire.

Historiographical discussions also have the potential of enriching citizenship education. They help students understand the vitality of the discipline and how we as citizens come to understand what various moments in history mean and then, where relevant, apply those understandings to the present. Considering the fact that high school often is the last time that a large percentage of Americans will take history classes before engaging society as adults, teachers have a duty to create intriguing historical lessons. These realities inform why history educators should do everything they can to engage and challenge pre-service teachers, high school teachers, and students to understand the discipline of history.[2]

ESTABLISHING THE BASELINE

As Andrews, Warren, and Cousins designed the project, they constructed pre- and post-assessments for the high school students to complete that included both Likert scale questions and narrative responses that required students to provide examples of what they claimed in the Likert questions. Here are the PCHS Historiography Questions Pre-Assessment questions:

Rate each item on the scale shown to indicate your level of agreement:

1. I am very interested in the study of history.
   a. Strongly agree
   b. Agree
   c. Uncertain
   d. Disagree
   e. Strongly disagree

2. I think that to study history everyone should understand historiography.
   a. Strongly agree
   b. Agree
   c. Unfamiliar with the term
   d. Disagree
   e. Strongly disagree

Rate the item on the scale shown to indicate your level of understanding:

3. My own understanding of historiography is_____.
   a. Excellent
   b. Above Average
   c. Average
   d. Below Average
   e. Very Poor

Provide a short answer for the following two questions:

4. Explain what historiography is by providing an example with your explanation.
5. Explain the value of historiography by providing an example of its impact on an area of historical research.

In 2011–2012, the pre-assessment questions were only administered to IB history students who were enrolled in the History of the Americas IB and Twentieth Century World IB classes. The total number of students in the first year study was 141, with full results for 102 students in the baseline. In the second year, 2012–2013, the baseline included freshman American History classes and the two IB courses for a total of 479 students who

100 *Creating Historical Thinking and Learning*

answered the pre-assessment survey. In the third year, 2013–2014, there were 170 responses from the freshmen only. The IB classes also took the pre-assessment in fall 2014. Sara Brown, the school librarian, has been an essential contributor to the project, monitoring student usage of existing sources, procuring new sources—especially relevant secondary sources and JSTOR—and administering the pre- and post-assessments.

Results from the pre-assessment have been revealing. In the first year, among the two classes surveyed, the IB History of the Americas was an elective class, and not surprisingly the statistics demonstrated that 87 percent of the students agreed or strongly agreed with the statement: "I am very interested in the study of history." In contrast, only 38 percent of those students in the required freshmen course responded as agree or strongly agree.

Whereas the first question was meant to establish a general benchmark about student interest in history as a discipline, the second and third Likert questions were constructed to gauge student dispositions about the need for understanding historiography generally and their own understanding specifically. Students' responses to the second question, "I think that to study history everyone should understand historiography," were revealing. This time the students in the elective class responded as agree or strongly agree 38 percent of the time, whereas 63 percent selected the third option, "unfamiliar with the term." In the required class, 81 percent of the respondents selected agreed or strongly agreed, whereas only 14 percent chose "unfamiliar with the term."

The second question was designed to understand the level of understanding and certitude on the part of high school students. "I think that to study history everyone should understand historiography" allowed students to express the value of a known area of study. Because they were given the opportunity in the response to state if they were "unfamiliar with the term," they exercised their judgment of what historiography is. This is why the responses to the third question are significant. In both the required and elective classes, a larger percentage of students claimed to have a level of personal understanding of historiography, whereas declaring that they were "unfamiliar with the term," in the second question. For instance, in the required class 63 percent of the students claimed to be unfamiliar, admitting no knowledge of the term, whereas 100 percent of the students, in the same class, claimed to have a personal level of understanding from very poor to excellent.

These results suggest that something is amiss. The placement of narrative responses in questions four and five was designed to illuminate the incongruities of the students' responses. The fourth question asks students to "explain what historiography is by providing an example with your explanation." Students' answers to this question add substance to any assertion made in answering the second question. For instance, if students were familiar with the term they could provide an example of the term, unless they

Students and Historiography 101

claimed unfamiliarity. The fifth question asks students to "explain the value of historiography by providing an example of its impact on an area of historical research." Students' responses to this question indicate what level of understanding they have by requiring them to provide an example of historiography's impact on research.

What did students have to say in their narrative responses?

In explaining historiography many of the responses fell into the following categories:

1. "I don't know what historiography is."
2. "Don't understand the term."
3. "I am not familiar with this term."
4. "No idea. I imagine that historiography is a sort of oral history. As in, it is the history told by the people who experience it."
5. "Historiography is the analysis of historical evidence, for example: It is known that Germany lost world war 2 [sic] but if you analyzed the ways in which they lost it would be considered historiography."

These responses show an absence of understanding, and even where examples were attempted, the result is an inability to explain by way of example. The number of responses by students that fell into a "naïve" understanding of historiography, or more accurately, an absence of understanding, suggests that most students were actually "unfamiliar" with the term.

The final question asked students to "Explain the value of historiography by providing an example of its impact on an area of historical research." Many of the responses were as follows:

1. "I don't know what historiography is."
2. "Don't understand the term."
3. "Again, I'm not familiar with this term."
4. "I don't know how to answer this."

It was fairly common for students like the last one to report "I don't know how to answer this," after having placed their level of knowledge as "average." Another student wrote that their level of understanding was "excellent," but then wrote "we should understand that all history that we know is only history that has been recorded, and we must realize that we only have someone else's documentation of an event." Aside from such budding attempts at deconstructionism, the number of students who responded with no level of understanding in the narrative portion helped us to establish an accurate baseline of the students' actual understanding of historiography.

102 *Creating Historical Thinking and Learning*

THE READINGS

Following the pre-assessment, each year the project moved into the distribution of the reading assignments in preparation for the panel discussion, led by the pre-intern teachers, which addressed the historiography of the civil rights movement in the GVSU-led portion of the project. The following section explains how the high school students engaged in disciplinary conversations with the GVSU pre-service teachers. Kent Baker's IB History of the Americas students were presented with readings from Stephen F. Lawson and Charles M. Payne's *Debating the Civil Rights Movement, 1945–1968,* published in 1998.[3] The readings are often assigned at the collegiate level and are challenging but still accessible to high school students. However, the amount of reading was lengthy for high school students. Payne's essay is forty pages long whereas Lawson's essay is forty-four pages. Rather than debating the "Short Civil Rights Movement" versus the "Long Civil Rights Movement," the professors and teachers decided to ask the IB students to investigate the historiography of civil rights from the "top down" and the "bottom up."

Lawson's essay, "Debating the Civil Rights Movement: The View from the Nation," explains the essential role of the federal government and national organizations in securing civil rights for African Americans. Supporters of this school of historiography do not ignore the role of individual agency or common people in general. Instead, this perspective offers a compelling narrative that explains the vital role of space. For Lawson and other like-minded historians, it was the presidency, Congress, the courts, and national organizations like the National Association for the Advancement of Colored People and the Southern Christian Leadership Council that created the vital space for grass roots organizations and individuals to maneuver and achieve success. In this narrative, without federal largesse, civil rights gains may have occurred but only after an extended period of time.

Payne's essay, "Debating the Civil Rights Movement: The View from the Trenches," offers a very different perspective. For Payne, and those who adhere to the historiography of the "bottom up," it is wrong to ascribe the centrality of causation to the federal government. Payne and others like him argue that presidents, Congress, courts, and national organizations often were guilty of foot dragging. One need only examine the reluctance of the Kennedy administration to act until after the successful march on Washington. Or indeed, the reluctance of the Eisenhower administration to act in Little Rock until after local residents, including school children, confronted the governor and local school and government officials. Common people created the space for presidents to act, not the other way around. The two perspectives provided students with a stark contrast and an active area of disagreement, especially because both historians' essays are lively, passionate, and well-argued.

STUDENTS' DISCUSSIONS OF HISTORIOGRAPHY

Because of the distance between Grand Valley State University and Portage Central, an added element to the study was examination of the advantages and disadvantages of technology in the classroom. In the first year of the project, GVSU students made one in-person visit to PCHS to meet the students who participated in the panel discussion; however, the discussion itself was conducted via the Internet. In the first year, IB students gathered in the media center as a group; in the second year, they again met in the media center but were placed in small groups of four or five isolated from one another. By dividing the groups in the second year, Andrews and Baker hoped to increase student participation with each other as well as with the pre-service teachers. Both Andrews and Baker noticed during the first year that whereas students were actively questioning and responding to the pre-service teachers, there could have been more involvement among students themselves. To that end, changing the instant messaging and video "chat" service from Oovoo to Google Hangout from year one to year two was a beneficial adaptation. This change allowed Andrews and Baker to assign individual groups their own independent windows, which would each be seen and heard by the group as a whole.

In the project's first two years, the pre-service teachers followed the same format with the high school students, an overview of the two authors, an open discussion of the readings, and concluded with a discussion of Civil Rights Movement historiography. After the pre-service teachers' overview presentation, high school students' responses suggested evidence of the pedagogical efficacy of historiography. Students addressed a number of facets of the civil rights movement from a historiographical perspective, including what historiography is, the explanatory powers of both top-down and bottom-up perspectives, and what various individuals, groups, and governmental bodies meant to the movement. This exercise revealed ways in which students can pursue history from a disciplinary perspective.

During the panel discussions, several high school students eagerly asked historiographical questions. Although they typically started with textbook definitions, many made comments that indicated they had developed a working understanding of this field's historiography. For example, during the discussion of which historiographical school best explained Dr. Martin Luther King, the students compared Lawson's and Payne's presentation of King's action. Most students adopted top-down perspectives about King, seeing him as the leader of SCLC, a powerful national organization driven by King's forceful personality. One student described King as a celebrity. Students also discussed Ella Baker, Fannie Lou Hamer, Ed Nixon, and Malcolm X. When asked to consider which school—top down or bottom up— they thought best explained these individuals and the groups to which they belonged, they often chose a combination. Discussions were energetic and even heated as students debated these perspectives.

104 *Creating Historical Thinking and Learning*

The panel discussion was the first time many of the students had contemplated Dr. King as a complicated historical figure. Payne asks the reader to consider how to categorize King. Was he the King of August 1963, the iconic figure of the "I Have a Dream" speech? Or was he the King of 1968, who questioned the government and its president over the Vietnam War, and the status of the poor, as he supported garbage workers in Memphis? The same was true of Rosa Parks. Students needed to rethink the period's presidents and their actions. For instance, they were forced to think why President Eisenhower acted in Little Rock as he did, how one accounts for President Kennedy's action, or inaction, and seen through this new lens, why President Johnson led or reacted to civil rights developments after Kennedy's death. Here too, students began to splinter into pockets of support over the top-down and bottom-up historiographies.

During the 2012 panel discussion, one student threw a wrench into a rather free-flowing conversation by asking a pointed question of the pre-service teachers. As he framed his question, you could tell that he had been weighing how the explanatory power of either school of history worked. "I understand how the top-down or bottom-up schools explain the role of leaders, groups, and the government, but how does either explain the riots in Detroit?" There was a long pause on the part of the pre-service teachers until one of them remarked without elaboration that he thought the bottom up best explained the event. There was no attempt to identify how the advocates of the top down would have explained the riots. The question came at the end of the hour, perhaps mercifully for the pre-service teachers.

NINTH-GRADE STUDENTS AND HISTORIOGRAPHY

In the spring of 2015 a non-honors ninth-grade U.S. history class was added to the expanded study, with the hopes of adding three more classes in 2015–2016. At PCHS, students have the option of taking a non-honors or honors U.S. history. Sue Hoffman, a teacher with thirty-five years of experience, agreed to let the GVSU pre-service teachers lead a classroom discussion on the historiography of the civil rights movement. The reading for this class was an essay taken from the series *Modern Problems in American History 1877 to the Present*. Students read John D. Skrentny's essay, titled "The Minority Rights Revolution: Top Down and Bottom Up."[4] From the title one can tell it is in keeping with the same historiographical elements as the IB classes, and whereas this reading too was taken from a college-level resource, the essay was shorter and more accessible for fourteen- and fifteen-year-old freshmen.

The four GVSU pre-service teachers—three women and one man—prepared a lesson plan with the understanding that the students would have read the essay and had just begun a unit on the civil rights movement. Sue's students were welcoming and relatively small in number—just seventeen

Students and Historiography 105

total—making the situation more manageable for the nervous college students. The pre-service teachers' strategy was to split the class up into groups to address four main discussion points. Students were given a specific topic to discuss in their groups, and then one of the pre-service teachers would help to facilitate a small group discussion. After five to seven minutes, the groups would meet together for a whole group discussion of the topic.[5]

The following narratives are derived from an audio transcript from the class during their discussion of the events surrounding school desegregation in Little Rock, Arkansas, in 1957.

Students were asked if anyone knew what had happened there.

Male Student 1: "Wasn't it down south where nine students tried to go to school and the 101st Airborne showed up and then the sheriff showed up to stop them or, something like that?"

After confirming the students' basic understanding of what happened, the pre-service teachers showed a brief segment of a documentary specifically addressing the parameters of the event with news clips and interviews from 1957. The students were then asked to discuss how either the top-down or bottom-up perspectives better explain the events at Little Rock. Each group developed a majority opinion. Minority views were also explained.

Female Student 2: "I thought it was from the top because the government sent the kids to the school because they couldn't just walk to school."
Female Student 3: "Well I thought it was bottom up because—"
Female Student 4: "We thought it was top down because the government had to come in to the school and protect them, so it was almost like saying you have to let those kids go to school here."

Reporting from the last group:

Female Student 5: "We thought it was top down too, because basically the government stepped in and helped them."[7]

Here it should be noted that there were rumblings from students who thought that it was bottom up because the people made the government step in, but they were not quite sure about the argument and let the top-down explanation stand. Nevertheless, students' discussion included efforts to employ elements of historical thinking, including interpretations and weighing evidence they have at their disposal. And whereas their skills were obviously novice, they also clearly enjoyed this type of inquiry and application of disciplinary theory.

During another portion of the class, students discussed the events surrounding Rosa Parks and the Montgomery bus boycott. In this exchange,

106   *Creating Historical Thinking and Learning*

students contemplated available evidence to address questions about historical agency. Students did not use the term *agency*, but they clearly considered it as they tried to account for how changes occurred.

Male Student 6:	"It was bottom up, because mainly the whole thing was organized by the people. It was organized for a long time, but when Rosa Parks was arrested it was put into motion. So, they like, made the boycott."
Male Student 7:	"Oh yeah, we thought it was bottom up too, because Rosa Parks was the spark for it, and then the bus drivers lost about 90 percent of the people that drove and that really brought it down. So the government pretty much changed that."
Female Student 8:	"It was bottom up because it was started by the people."

One of the pre-service teachers then asked another student to share her views. During the small group discussion, she indicated that she thought that the bus boycott was best explained through the top-down historiography.

Female Student 9:	"It could be top down because the government made the segregation laws and then she was just there, and they (African Americans) didn't have power." However, some students voiced the opinion that the movement could not be top down because people made the difference.[8]

As the debate shifted to legislation and the Civil Rights Acts of 1964, 1965, and 1968 the explanatory power of one school of historiography over another was not quite so clear or satisfying. Greater numbers of students started to insist that it was both top down and bottom up. Interestingly, the ninth-grade students tried to combine these historiographical schools in a way that was similar to how the IB students had. Clearly, there is no historiographical consensus on this issue, and significantly, this is reflected in both the ninth-grade and IB students' ideas. In both settings, students wrestled in a meaningful way with causation at a deeper level than they normally would. They also enjoyed discussing this historiography and developed a more acute understanding of history as a discipline.

CONCLUSION

Those who criticize historiography's use in high schools generally express two main concerns. First, they assert that the material is too difficult for secondary students. The PCHS historiography project's findings suggest that this concern is unsubstantiated. Second, they question the purpose of this type of disciplinary inquiry, asking if the schools should try to produce historians. This too appears misplaced given students' budding success with disciplinary aspects of history. Whereas historiography can indeed be complicated and nuanced, a major task of history educators to make these confusing aspects of history intellectually palatable for students. All students need to be reminded that interpretive understandings can't be "Googled." Introducing historiographical debates allows high school students the opportunity think deeply and critically about what really matters in the discipline.

Additionally regarding the second concern, scholars like Peter Lee have directly confronted this critique. In his essay, "Understanding History," Lee refutes the faulty notion that the disciplinary aspects of history, those he classifies as "second order" skills, compared to the knowledge-level skills, which he categorizes as "first order," are too difficult. He states that, "What is at stake is not the training of mini-historians, but changing students' understanding of history." Studying historiography lifts the veil that occludes the interest of many secondary students, allowing them to peer into, and participate in, the vital debates among historians over causality and meaning. The experiences of the PCHS students lend credence to not only Lee's perspectives but also Caroline Hoefferle's. She notes, "We do our students a disservice if we represent history as a noncontroversial presentation of 'the facts.'"[6]

If the PCHS project has provided many areas of promise for the use of historiography in the classroom, it has also pointed to some areas of concern. Many students, for example, want to place one school of historiography in either the right or wrong category rather than challenge the explanatory power of each by thinking deeply about causation. Admittedly, some of this was due to the fact that panel discussions were confined to a fifty-minute period. There was also a tendency among the high school students to simply select top down, or bottom up, provide an example that they thought fit, like Little Rock, and let the assertion lie as a prima facie argument. Instead, students need to be led into a discussion of the evidence that Lawson and Payne used in their essays. As is true of many historical debates, their perspectives were fundamentally arguments over who was creating space within which the other party could operate. Asking students to expound on those arguments went a long way toward enhancing their understanding of the discipline, and creating more interest in history, enriching their experiences in the classroom.

The post-assessment data from 2011–12, 2012–13, and 2013–14 show an improvement in interest in terms of the Likert scale scores. Encouragingly, the results to this point demonstrate that the use of historiography does increase interest and does lead to a deeper level of historical thinking on the part of high school students. For instance, one student response to "explain what historiography is by providing an example with your explanation,"

108 *Creating Historical Thinking and Learning*

was, "Historiography is the study of how history changes with new perspectives and developments over time. For example, the causes and effecrts [sic] of World War I have changed since the war has occurred. People know that Germany's militarism is not the only reason that the war occurred." Students' scores and narratives also suggest that they gained a general appreciation of historiography. For example, when asked to "Explain the value of historiography by providing an example of its impact on an area of historical research," a student responded by saying that, "Historiography is very important when studying an area in history due to the fact that it provides the researcher with various perspectives, allowing him to formulate his own view. This applies to research of the history of civil rights in the US because there are many different factors that have impacted the accomplishments of the Civil Rights Movement."[7]

NOTES

1. Fritz Fischer, "The Historian as Translator: Historical Thinking, the Rosetta Stone of History Education," *Historically Speaking* 12:3(2011), 15–17.
2. U.S. Census, http://www.census.gov/hhes/socdemo/education/data/cps/2014/tables.html (accessed April 28, 2015); and Jonathan Kozol quoted in Jarrett Dapier, "Back to School in the Bronx," *In These Times* 36:11(2012), 34–35 http://inthesetimes.com/article/14027/back_to_school_in_the_bronx (accessed May 5, 2015).
3. Stephen F. Lawson and Charles M. Payne, ed., *Debating the Civil Rights Movement, 1945–1968* (Lanham, MD: Rowman and Littlefield, 1998).
4. John D. Skrentny, "The Minority Rights Revolution: Top Down and Bottom Up," in *Major Problems in American History: Volume II: Since 1865*, ed. Elizabeth Cobbs Hoffman, Edward J. Blum, and Jon Gjerde (Boston: Wadsworth Cengage Learning, 2002), 313–35.
5. Sue Hoffman's Ninth-Grade U.S. History Class, student responses to Civil Rights Historiography, March 27, 2015, audio recording in Andrews's possession.
6. Peter Lee, "Understanding History," in *Theorizing Historical Consciousness*, ed. Peter Sexias (Toronto: University of Toronto Press, 2004), 129–64; and Caroline Hoefferle, "Teaching Historiography to High School and Undergraduate Students," *Magazine of History* 21:2(2007), 41.
7. Post-assessment data, Kent Baker's class results, 2013–2014.

10 Collaboration and Pre-Service Teachers
Using Historiography as Pedagogy

Pre-service history teachers encounter challenges unfamiliar to students of other disciplines. Their programs encourage exposure to wide-ranging historical content and educational methods, whereas their professors demand advanced competence in reading, writing, and research. Capstone history methods courses bridge the gap between these parallel but overlapping goals; here students pass from comprehension to application and begin creating their own approaches to the material. But as they near the end of their curriculum, the burdens of professional readiness—the need to master what is most practical—sometimes complicates these courses and obscures the relationship between content and theory. In the rush to prepare for their first teaching assignments, pre-service teachers are less likely to see the forest for the trees and move beyond a rudimentary understanding of lesson design. WMU's teacher education program is no different. History 4940, a one-semester secondary education methods class completed just before intern teaching, becomes the first real opportunity for pre-service teachers to develop pedagogical approaches. Authenticity remains one of the central goals of this course; instructors reinforce the benefits of historical inquiry in the hopes that students will incorporate these ideas into their own lessons.[1]

The collaborative partnership with PCHS has reinforced these connections by helping students rethink the importance of applied theory. Each semester, pre-service teachers from History 4940 introduce historiography to PCHS's International Baccalaureate (IB) history courses. For the past several years, the course has been taught in alternate semesters by Wilson Warren and James Cousins. This chapter explains James Cousins's approaches to the course regarding students' participation in the PCHS historiography project. The course's lessons articulate and apply historical theory to classroom content in a way that benefits both students and pre-service teachers alike. PCHS students develop deeper connections with the material, appreciate the complexity of the historical process, and begin to understand the diversity of scholarship; pre-service teachers solidify the connections between content and theory while they expand the potential of future lessons. The following retraces the recent history of the project in a narrative of successes and setbacks. Lessons learned in one semester were applied,

110   *Creating Historical Thinking and Learning*

assessed, and reworked for the next semester. It is a process that can never be perfected but has helped clarify the goals for the methods course and improved my approach to teaching historiography.

At WMU, students enter History 4940 after passing through graduated coursework. They gain increasing levels of historiographic sophistication. Baseline concepts from introductory courses provide foundations for topic and theme-specific historiography discussed in advanced, writing-intensive history courses. By the time they reach History 4940, pre-service teachers should have the ability to frame useful historical questions, choose meaningful primary and secondary sources, model historical reading and writing, support independent research projects, and think deeply about the uses and meanings of history. My initial approach to History 4940 developed with an idea to lay pedagogy on top of preexisting or slightly rebuilt foundations, complementing abilities learned over the length of their program.

Classroom activities, assessments, and discussions in the early weeks of my first semester undermined this strategy. In some cases, students possessed a reasonable grasp of method and content but were unable to express concepts related to historical theory or to see individual works as part of larger body of historical writing. More generally, I found that students lacked an ability to interpret historical writing, to understand the nuance of historical arguments, and to see that two competing ideas could exist in the same topic. They all had demonstrable experience—in analyzing primary sources, comparing the works of academic historians, and conducting their own research projects—but lacked the ability to translate these habits into teachable content.

My hopes at shoring up small deficiencies became less reasonable, and the question became one of practicality—that is, how I could give pre-service teachers enough historical awareness to seal the rift between comprehension and application. For this I fell back on the works of Caroline Hoefferle, who recommended a theory-driven approach to teaching historiography; Robert Green Jr., who developed historical thinking in high school through secondary source comparisons; and Thomas Fallace, who encouraged pre-service teachers to do the same. Readings, activities, and in-class discussions of historiography were limited to one week, three fifty-minute classes, of a sixteen-week semester. I divided that week into two parts. Part one began with an overview of major historiographic schools: annals, Marxist, "Great Man" history, social history, microhistory, and others. I then asked students to identify theoretical positions, presenting them with selections from E. P. Thompson's *The Making of the English Working Class*, a social history of Victorian England; George Ostrogorsky's *History of the Byzantine State*, a Marxist interpretation of the later Roman Empire; and Peter Thompson's *Rum Punch and Revolution*, a cultural history of pre-Revolutionary American politics.[2]

In part two, students developed a comparative reading assignment to complement a unit on the American Revolution, in this way demonstrating

Collaboration and Pre-Service Teachers 111

the importance of theory to the process of secondary source analysis. They were to locate a key point of scholarly debate, find relevant sources within that debate, and design a classroom activity around excerpted readings and questions. Post-activity discussions exposed an unanticipated level of unfamiliarity, both with theory and the relationship of theory to the historical process. Unsurprisingly, pre-service teachers struggled to see how a discussion of historiography might benefit their students; most found it an interesting but inconsequential aside. Their impressions of part two were couched in similar terms. Those able to locate secondary sources found it difficult to translate these selections into teachable content. The problem hinged on a disconnect between our review of historical theory and the application of theory to pedagogy. Historiography remained an abstraction, something rarified and reserved for academic historians. Only a few understood how they could build lessons that reflected authentic historical research.

My decision to participate in the PCHS historiography project grew out of these frustrated attempts, and I discussed plans for integrating pre-service teachers from my Spring 2013 semester methods course into PCHS's IB program. Pre-service teacher participants worked together to create a single lesson plan but delivered it in separate, two- to three-person groups. That semester, students from the senior-level twentieth century world history class learned about the origins and rule of single-party states; four pre-service teachers, working in groups of two, were to facilitate lessons on the rise of the Chinese Communist Party (CCP). Wilson Warren and I decided on a comparative reading activity and selected excerpts from Charles Fitzgerald's 1976 *Mao Tse Tung and China* and from Rebecca Karl's 2010 biography, *Mao Zedong and China in the Twentieth-Century World*. Both offered distinct interpretations of Mao Tse Tung's role in the creation of the Chinese Communist Party.[3]

Fitzgerald and Karl approached Mao from different perspectives and offered divergent explanations of historical causation. For Fitzgerald, Mao had "exceptional qualities" based, not on hereditary but his "personal ascendancy," a self-propelled will developed as a child in the Hunan Province, the revolutionary mind-set he developed in early adulthood, and the political charisma he found as young librarian at Peking University. Mao was not a product of his revolutionary environment but its catalyst. His authority was "not formally defined by any statue of the Communist state which is so largely his own creation."

Rebecca Karl turned Fitzgerald's interpretation on its head, interpreting Mao as an almost coincidental reflection of larger social and political movements. Mao was an "impressive and effective organizer," but the CCP was not his creation. Revolutionary momentum was organic; it began with peasant farmers and soldiers and was brought to fruition by the massacre of striking railway workers in February of 1923, the ruthless suppression of Chinese protestors in May 1925, and Comintern agents sent by Stalin to unify Chinese nationalists and communists. Mao was swept along in a

112   *Creating Historical Thinking and Learning*

current of revolutionary fervor, and his February 1927 report presented to CCP leaders challenged them to join or suffer the consequences of inaction.

The timing of guest teaching appearances, mixed with the completion of other course objectives, added another level of complexity. In place of lectures on theoretical schools, an approach attempted during the previous semester, I focused exclusively on comparative source analysis and focused class discussion on Fitzgerald and Karl. Selected chapters became jumping-off points for discussions of credibility, authorial perspective, date of publication, and the use of close reading. Participants in the PCHS project developed lesson plans that tied readings into larger discussions of historiography. Put simply, they were encouraged to mimic the process outlined in class. But first drafts were devoid of interpretive content, and students focused on details from Mao's upbringing, education, and travels: when he left home, how and with whom he conspired, and other incidents. The purpose, as they explained it, was superior to our class activities because it allowed students to evaluate sources according to points of agreement and disagreement. Karl drew Mao's wife into the story but left out his early childhood; Fitzgerald discussed Mao's university career but excluded mention of Stalin's Comintern agents. Both authors felt the unification of Chinese Nationalists and peasant workers were important components of the story. And because they seemed dispassionate in these accounts, that aspect of the narrative was considered the most authentic.

In this way, they confused rudimentary primary source analysis with a close reading of secondary sources. Their exercise might have helped IB students digest the material but would not enhance a greater understanding of historical thinking. We began again, this time with special attention to historical causation. They revised their plans and structured activities around historical theories as I previously suggested. They started with a brief history of historiography, progressing from "great man" theory, as represented by Fitzgerald, and closed with a summary of social history, exemplified by Rebecca Karl. Their goal, as they explained it, was to help IB students recognize Fitzgerald's work as an outmoded historical scheme that was outdone by Karl's more recent social historical approach.

This was closer to the mark but still missed the point. In promoting Karl over Fitzgerald, students still operated under the assumption that there was correct version of history and that the scholarly tradition of a particular field is one ceaseless march toward the narrative perfected. This is one step removed from treating textbooks as unimpeachable final authorities. The final days before their appearances left little time for substantial revisions, and they proceeded into their guest lecture appearances with only a few suggestions for improvement.

The benefit of teaching to a class of high-achieving, college-bound high school seniors is that optional readings are rarely optional. Pre-service teachers arrived to classes of twenty-five to thirty energetic, talkative, and for the most part, well-prepared high school seniors. They began by asking

Collaboration and Pre-Service Teachers 113

students to consider the term *historiography*, breaking down word origins and defining its present use as the "study of, the study of history." From here the conversation shifted to Mao and Chinese Communism, with special attention to Mao's decision to enter the Communist party. A KWL activity reinforced connections between Chinese and Russian Communism and laid the groundwork for a more general exploration of Marxist ideology. Students approached Karl and Fitzgerarld through guided readings with discussion questions keyed to large, paragraph-length excerpts. IB students were asked to consider the "historiographic differences" between readings and again, about how publication dates influenced our impressions of the readings. They considered whether the understanding of history changes from generation to generation; the goal of the pre-service teachers was to demonstrate how dated historical interpretations sometimes lead to historically inaccurate observations.

On balance, their reception was positive. Exit slips showed that students carried away a marginally improved sense of historical complexity, and the majority seemed to understand that professional historians could and do often disagree on certain aspects of the past. However, their lesson failed to capture the most essential and theoretically relevant qualities of the readings. Authorial perspective, the use of source evidence, and the significance of historical causality, as it related to Mao and the CCP, were never addressed. Moreover, by placing these works in direct competition with one another, IB students were taught that professional history is inherently adversarial, that historians write only to correct erroneous versions of the past. Finally, by passing over the idea of a secondary source tradition, students missed the opportunity to recognize the most important aspect of historical scholarship: significance. Introducing students to the concept of historical significance would have helped build an appreciation for the dynamic and robust nature of the discipline; it might also have shown that whereas historical research is sometimes lonely, it is never solitary.

These experiences led me to rethink my approach not just to the project but to the entire History 4940 course. I narrowed my field of focus and considered how I might communicate the most essential qualities of historiography. And so rather than ad-hoc interjections forced within the space of a single week, I decided to introduce the subject by way of historical thinking and designed a series of units in support of specific and readily teachable principles. Historical questions supported lessons on corroboration, significance, and perspective; I spent less time with the abstract historical theory or schools of historical research and focused on close analytical readings of individual secondary sources and left readings from Karl and Fitzgerald out of these discussions. Lectures, readings, and activities were designed to assist pre-service teachers in the integration of historical thinking.

To begin our unit on corroboration I asked, "Who bears responsibility for the fall of the Roman Republic?" Students read selections from Claude Nicolet's *The World of the Citizen in Republican Rome*, Christian Meier's

114 *Creating Historical Thinking and Learning*

biography of Julius Caesar, and Ronald Syme's *Roman Revolution*. Each historian attributed the fall to distinctive factors: Nicolet argued that first-century military reforms separated Roman soldiers from general citizenry; Christian Meier cited the decadence of Roman patronage and believed the search for status compelled a desire for war; Ronald Syme placed the blame on large aristocratic families who steered the Republic away from sound government. Students had no difficulty locating points of disagreement but struggled to find corroboration. I asked how these authors approached the question, the types of sources they cited, and the subjects they considered most relevant. Most agreed that Nicolet, Meier, and Syme emphasized social class and looked for, and consequently found, tensions between competing social groups. From here we moved into a general discussion of histori-cal significance and reflected on the pursuit of useful, historically signifi-cant research questions. My students agreed that the most useful questions originated from incorporating diverse but complementary historical inter-pretations. They applied this logic to the creation of a historical research assignment and developed topics and source bibliographies appropriate to grades six to ten.[4]

I presented my unit on perspective in a similar fashion and with a focus on application, how authorial perspective influences interpretations of pri-mary sources, and how these same principles translate to effective history pedagogy. Excerpts from Fernand Braudel's *Structures of Everyday Life*, the first in a three-part history of early modern Europe, and Carlo Ginzberg's *The Cheese and the Worms*, presented them with drastically different but equally compelling histories. Braudel, a historian of the annals school, pulled together a vast assortment of textual and non-textual sources—weather data, population statistics, documents, and other records—to create a com-plex but convincing macro history of the fourteenth through eighteenth cen-turies. Ginzberg, a cultural historian of the same period, focused his efforts on the life of Domenico Scandella, an Italian miller declared a heretic in the Italian Inquisition. The difference was one of perspective. Braudel believed that the foundations of everyday life floated on larger currents of environ-mental and political change. Ginzberg approaches the realities of everyday life through the life of an individual and draws the life of Scandella into a larger cultural narrative. I presented students with both works and asked them to think through the implications. How could a lesson on antebellum slavery, the Revolutions of 1848, or the Byzantine theme system benefit from a micro or macro perspective? Only at the conclusion of these activities did we then consider readings from Fitzgerald and Karl. This time, instead of focusing on comparative differences or the progress toward historical accuracy, students looked for signs of authorial perspective and conjectured about significance.[5]

I approached the PCHS project in spring 2014 with greater confidence in my pre-service teachers, expecting they would take from in-class dis-cussions and relate the same principles, of corroboration, perspective,

Collaboration and Pre-Service Teachers 115

and significance, to their IB classrooms. They were divided into pairs and instructed to build lessons around the same readings but after this were left to their own devices, creating their own big ideas, lesson objectives, essential questions, and lesson outlines. The results were mixed. Group A introduced their lesson as "thinking like a historian" and prompted students to identify the purposes, values, and limitations of each reading. From here they moved into a content-driven lecture on the origins of Communism and China's involvement in World War II. But the bulk of their lesson focused on historical perspective, and by way of example, they assigned groups of IB students to one of several historical traditions—social, cultural, military, Marxist, and gender history. They provided students with an excerpt of Mao Zedong's 1927 "Report on the Investigation of the Peasant Movement in Hunan" and asked the IB students to interpret the speech through their assigned tradition, mirroring the perspective introduced at the outset. Members of the class reported findings, and the class discussed strengths and weaknesses of each position. IB students returned to the initial question and began to move through the central concepts of primary source criticism— credibility, context, and correlation. Pre-service teachers asked, do historians shape the past or simply record it? Is it more important for historians to provide a dispassionate reading or a creative interpretation of evidence?

Members of Group B felt students required even greater exposure to content and began with a lecture on Mao's participation in the CCC, the revolt of 1927, and the Chinese Civil War. This was followed by a conversation about authorial bias, and students were asked to consider how bias influences the interpretation of primary sources. A "tweet-based" activity contributed to their main idea. The class read a series of 140-character tweets created using one of Mao's earliest public speeches and were told to compose individual "re-tweets" that captured the essence and intention of the entire string. They did this alone, then in groups, and were asked to come together to share points of agreement and disagreement. Some of the prompts for this discussion included: What did individual members leave out of their tweets and why? What did the group consider to be most essential? Pre-service teachers summarized the activity by explaining that historical scholarship is never truly complete and that the historical narrative is built on selectivity and perspective. To reinforce these ideas, Group B provided students with biographical sketches of both Fitzgerald and Karl then asked if personal or cultural differences influenced their writing. In their application activity, IB students were instructed to underline phrases from the excerpts in an effort to root out cultural biases. They considered the meaning of individual words and if the choice of vocabulary had a significant influence on their larger arguments.

Exit slips demonstrated successes and deficiencies in both presentations. Group A asked, "What does it mean to think like a historian?" and students reflected on the value of primary source analysis, the role of theoretical perspectives, and the necessity of recognizing authorial bias. One

116   *Creating Historical Thinking and Learning*

student responded: "Thinking like a historian means that you question different interpretations as opposed to just believing them." Others focused on analysis and concluded that historians "must evaluate every aspect about a source" or "must constantly question and analyze." Only a few described the process of corroboration and considered history as a "learning process" that is refined over time. More decided history was an arduous task. "It is your duty," one student remarked, "to analyze all those interpretations and piece together your own interpretation."

Group B posed an open-ended question asking students to record two or three interesting facts learned from the day's activities. In their responses, students focused less on historiography and more on their content lecture, the "ideas of the CCP," labor unions, nationalism, and "Mao's family." They remained silent on the benefits of the tweet activity, the selection of primary sources, and questions related to interpretive bias. The problem may have been in the delivery of content and the application of theory. By separating historical content from the interpretation of that content, Group B treated theory as abstract, largely irrelevant conjecture. The few who referenced Karl and Fitzgerald described only the content of their work, not the method of its construction.

Lessons from this semester were closer to the mark but left room for improvement. A concentrated approach to historiography helped pre-service teachers recognize the value of historical thinking and link theory to application but left no room for historical content. Both groups struggled to find appropriate places for the history of Chinese Communism and jumped awkwardly between a textbook-driven narrative of the early twentieth century and the theories of Karl and Fitzgerald. They passed these confusions on to the IB students, who recognized the hard work of historians and the established political history of China but with no connection between the two. This was the unfortunate result of my approach to the subject and my insistence on teachable material based on authentic inquiry, but created examples out of thin air and without a basis in historical content.

In the most recent semester with the project I looked for a less synthetic manner of instruction in History 4940. I restricted the discussion of theoretical schools and promoted historiography through a series of in-class activities. Each demonstrated a small piece of a larger historiographic puzzle but developed in the course of content-driven lectures and activities. The intention was to model the skills of historiography and authentic historical inquiry but in way that complemented traditional content standards. I presented these activities in a series of ten-minute lessons on Early Republic.

The first exercise began with a lecture on the Stamp Act crises of 1765. I interpreted these revolts as a means of political activism and placed them within the context of Bacon's Rebellion in Virginia (1676), Coode's Rebellion in Maryland (1689), Cary's Rebellion in North Carolina (1709–11), and the anti-impressment riots of Boston (1747). I distributed two primary sources related to the Stamp Act—Benjamin Franklin's speech before

British Parliament and Thomas Hutchinson's account of mob violence. They were asked to read these sources and write brief, one-paragraph answers to the question, "How were the Stamp Act riots justified?" using these sources as the basis of their answers. I collected and redistributed these summaries along with a series of questions: What sources does the author privilege? How does the author interpret historical causation? And how does your interpretation differ from the author's?

I took these understandings a step further during my lesson on the influences and motivations of antebellum Southern plantation owners, New England merchants, and Pennsylvania farmers. I discussed each group in detail, with special attention to "definable characteristics," and then distributed primary sources that complicated or directly contradicted my accounts. I asked students to read and discuss the validity of these sources and consider how they might fit within my narrative; should they be given greater weight than other examples? Should the entire lecture be rewritten to accommodate? I closed by doing just that, symbolically inserting their ideas within the body of the lecture outline. We closed with a discussion of why they included or excluded individual sources.

The intention of these activities was to help pre-service teachers build a progressive understanding of historiography but in content-driven examples. Through my lesson on the Stamp Act, I hoped to expose students to the influences of personal historical perspective—that individuals approach history from with unique, often unexpressed, viewpoints and attitudes. My goal for the second lesson was to have students move beyond contradictory and revisionist historical arguments and understand the collaborative nature of the profession.

I began preparations for the PCHS project in spring 2015 with greater confidence but decided to return to a collaborative, directed lesson plan. My students returned to Karl and Fitzgerald as the basis of the day's activities and designed a more content-driven approach to historiography and the concept of authorial perspective; lectures and classroom activities attempted to create a more organic, primary source–driven explanation of historical thinking. To accomplish this, pre-service teachers elected for a more open-ended discussion format. IB students developed individual interpretations of Mao's 1937 interview with British journalist James Bertram, and through this, reflected on their own biases. This led to questions about the influences, attitudes, and theories of Fitzgerald, Karl, and other professional historians. This was a more useful approach but exposed other weaknesses, namely a lack of familiarity with advanced concepts. They knew enough to ask questions but could not facilitate productive discussions. IB students provided constructive responses to questions related to the selection and interpretations of primary sources, the benefits and limitations of secondary sources, corroboration, and perspective, but were unable to unite or extend individual insights. The result was an improved but necessarily incomplete understanding.

118   *Creating Historical Thinking and Learning*

My participation in the PCHS historiography project has been an invaluable guide to my own misconceptions. I know now that a failure to impart a balanced and refined understanding of historiography may have lasting repercussions, not simply in the context of a single lesson but over the course of an entire teaching career. Historiography allows early-career teachers to communicate the complex, intellectually rich basis of our profession in a meaningful way. In doing so, they become better models of historical reading skills, better prepared to assess student research and writing, and better able to connect historical content to contemporary issues.

NOTES

1. For a summary of the department's curriculum development, see Linda J. Borish, Mitch Kachun, and Cheryl Lyon-Jenness, "Rethinking a Curricular 'Muddle in the Middle': Revising the Undergraduate History Major at Western Michigan University," *Journal of American History* 95:4(2009), 1102–13.
2. Caroline Hoefferle, "Teaching Historiography to High School and Undergraduate Students," *Magazine of History* 21:2(2007), 40–44; Robert Green Jr., "Reconstruction Historiography: A Source of Teaching Ideas," *The Social Studies* 82:4(1991), 153–57; Thomas D. Fallace, "Historiography and Teacher Education: Reflections on an Experimental Course," *The History Teacher* 42:2(2009), 205–22; E.P. Thompson, *The Making of the English Working Class* (New York: Vintage Books, 1966); George Ostrogorsky, *History of the Byzantine State* (New Brunswick, NJ: Rutgers University Press, 1969); and Peter Thompson, *Rum Punch and Revolution: Taverngoing and Public Life in Eighteenth-Century Philadelphia* (Philadelphia: University of Pennsylvania Press, 1998).
3. Charles P. Fitzgerald, *Mao Tse-Tung and China* (New York: Penguin Books, 1977); George Ostrogorsky, *History of the Byzantine State* (New Brunswick, NJ: Rutgers University Press, 1969); and Rebecca E. Karl, *Mao Zedong and China in the Twentieth-Century World: A Concise History* (Durham, NC: Duke University Press, 2010).
4. Claude Nicolet, *The World of the Citizen in Republican Rome* (Berkley: University of California Press, 1980); Christian Meier, *Caesar: A Biography* (New York: Basic Books, 1969); and Ronald Syme, *The Roman Revolution* (London: Oxford University Press, 2002).
5. Fernand *Braudel, The Structures of Everyday Life: The Limits of the Possible* (New York: Harper and Row, 1981); and Carlo Ginzburg, *The Cheese and the Worms: The Cosmos of a Sixteenth-Century Miller* (Baltimore: Johns Hopkins University Press, 1992).

11 Alternative Education
Historiography and Historical Thinking in the Nontraditional Classroom

Over ten thousand alternative "at-risk" or remedial high schools now operate in the United States.[1] Research in this area has expanded in recent years but remains confined to the observation, diagnosis, and management of student behavior, methods of student retention, or approaches to remedial education. What is lacking is serious discussion of curriculum and more specifically, how alternative programs might benefit from distinctly non-remedial content. The history classroom provides a unique opportunity to test this assumption as course materials and assessments here contribute to a false perception of utility among students. The following presents the results of a one-year pilot program administered by WMU's James Cousins, which introduced historiography into the U.S. history curriculum of two Kalamazoo-area alternative high schools, Barclay Hills Educational Center and the Climax-Scotts Adult Alternative Education Program. Over the course of the 2013–14 academic year, students received multiple exposures to the historian's craft—activities designed to increase their familiarity with source analysis, research methodology, and historiography. I coordinated my instruction with Mr. Terry Butcher, a fifteen-year veteran of alternative education who splits his time between the two programs and delivered six half-hour historiography lessons at each school. Preliminary results make a compelling case not only for the inclusion of advanced content in alternative programs but also for a differentiated approach to student-directed research.

Alternative schooling, broadly conceived, has long been part of American education; alternative methods of instruction were shaped and reshaped in response to mainstream educational practices. The early nineteenth-century vocational methodology of Johann Pestalozzi and monitorial system of Joseph Lancaster fit within this tradition, as did larger, publicly funded Progressive Era reforms. Alternative education gathered momentum in the 1960s with the expansion of theory-driven elite private schools, the proliferation of home schools, and new publicly funded opportunities provided under the Elementary and Secondary Education Act of 1965. The first alternative public high schools were established in this same period and with the goal of providing safe, enriching experiences for children and young adults

120   *Creating Historical Thinking and Learning*

with cognitive or emotional disabilities. In recent years, alternative public schools shifted their focus to "at-risk" students who, because of a variety social, behavior, or environmental concerns, are less likely to graduate from traditional programs. As a result, the significance of alternative education is now promoted as an extension of potential economic benefits, represented in the billons lost in taxes and wages.[2]

In Michigan, 369 alternative programs serve close to twenty-five thousand students, but advocacy, as well as funding, is on the decline as preschool education, afterschool programs, and online courses assume larger portions of attention and state funding. Both schools in this study face significant financial challenges. Barclay Hills, serving the Parchment School District, has an enrollment of 135 students ages fifteen through twenty-one. The program at Climax-Scotts is smaller, with close to forty-five matriculates, but serves a wider age range with students as young as fifteen and as old as sixty in the same classroom. Age-related differences are the result of district funding models; each school receives roughly $8,000 per year, per student up to the age of twenty, after which time funding drops to $300. At Barclay, students are dematriculated the semester following their twenty-first birthday, whereas students at Climax-Scotts may continue indefinitely.[3]

These are, generally speaking, programs of last resort, the result of behavioral issues and after multiple expulsions from their local high school. Some are there under court order and "tethered" or restricted to campus grounds during the school day, with movements tracked via ankle bracket. All are working toward the completion of a high school diploma and following the curriculum and content standards set forward by the state of Michigan. This is seen as a more attractive path than the GED, which has increased in difficulty in recent years.

In preliminary discussions with Mr. Butcher, I tried to get a sense of the educational climate and how or if the circumstances of enrollment affected student interaction, learning outcomes, or expectations. Student discipline and the management of disruptive behavior is, Mr. Butcher noted, a significant problem but slightly less important than basic issues of literacy. Lower levels of reading comprehension have altered his approach to every aspect of his class. Group work, lectures, in-class activities, and reading assignments are all constructed to educate students on how to be educated, explaining how students can record and then interpret classroom lectures and in-class readings. Butcher begins each lesson with content vocabulary, "anti-Semitism," "tariff," "dictator," etc., alongside basic vocabulary of potentially confusing words necessary for historical context. In-class readings are drawn almost entirely from secondary sources written at a sixth- to eighth-grade reading level. When assigning independent reading, Butcher relies on reading guides to direct student attention. Questions prompt responses, and reading sessions are limited to five minutes or less.

I was also told that discussion, video clips, and interactive group projects worked best and that students who felt ignored were more likely to cause disruptions or simply lose focus. And so I began with a fairly obvious challenge—how could I present text-based historical theory without using a text? The problem required me to rethink my expectations for historical literacy and the benefits of comparative historical analysis. Rather than using a combination of historical sources to prove a distant, abstract point, I decided to reverse the process, asking students to consider the why, not the how. I hoped relatively simple questions might then build to larger and more complex interpretations, piquing historical curiosity and encouraging, not defending an interest in historical reading. Classroom activities encouraged complex understandings of history and in the process, defined concepts and practices important to historiography. My plan was to begin with basic definitions, primary vs. secondary sources, perspective, and narrative before progressing to historical causation, significance, truth in history, and ultimately historical theory. Through this I hoped to build a bottom-up appreciation of the historical process, in this way creating a natural, self-evident space for more abstract principles. Not every exercise was successful. Some fell flat, some stumbled because of limited participation, and a few were suspended because of behavioral issues. I hoped the cumulative effect of my visits and activities would have a measurable influence that could be quantified by my final assessment survey or through Mr. Butcher's direct observations.

I began in early October with a pre-test that asked students to answer four open-ended questions. They would: 1) define the purpose of history and 2) describe the job of the professional historian. Questions three and four were related but more abstract: 3) can historians have different interpretations of the past yet be similarly correct? and 4) does our understanding of history change over time? Answers to the first question were predictable. Most agreed that the purpose of history was to "learn about the past," "to know what happened," or "to know how we got to where we are today." And for many, the job of the professional historian was equally uncomplicated: "to teach," to "tell or talk about the past," or simply to "study history." When asked if historians could have different yet similarly valid interpretations, most answered in the affirmative but saw these difference as a matter of opinion. In the words of one student, "Everyone [has] different opinions and understanding[s]." Students were somewhat confused by the question of interpretive change and again related historical research to opinion, as though the only change in historical research is our opinion of it.

A week later we began with an activity titled "sources from sources." Groups of three or four gathered around a central "primary source," a student who was asked to retell a meaningful story from his or her childhood. Others in the group were considered "secondary sources" and were told only to listen, not to interact with their primary counterpart. At the conclusion of the story, those students assigned to be secondary sources completed fifteen-word summaries. However, they did not have the benefit of more contact with the primary source. Class discussion began with questions about this limitation; students complained that fifteen words were simply

122 Creating Historical Thinking and Learning

not enough to accurately summarize the story in detail. Their responses allowed us to consider a deeper question of data collection, how historians gather, distill, and then communicate the past. We discussed the idea that historians are selective and extract only that information they consider important, that historians make reasonable assumptions of historical value and interpret this value not through opinion but evidence.

I then asked each secondary source to read their summary aloud, whereas the primary source, the originator of the story, sat and reflected on its veracity. The primary source was instructed to remain silent during this activity but rate each response on a scale of one to ten, one being a highly inaccurate summary and ten a perfect retelling; most responses were evaluated at between two and four. For the third part of the exercise, secondary sources worked together to synthesize their individual summaries into a single twelve-word summary. Group members enjoyed debating the relative merits of their own work and argued for the inclusion of particular ideas into the group summary. At the end of their debates, I asked secondary sources to deliver this combined "revisionist history" to the primary source and asked the primary source to evaluate their revision. Most revisionist summaries scored between six and eight despite disagreement and truncated word limitations.

I closed the activity by asking secondary sources to consider how their summaries might be clarified or improved: What information is missing? What would allow you to better capture the feelings and intentions of the storyteller? How might an expanded context improve our understanding? Students acting as secondary sources returned to their primary sources and discussed not just the literal meanings of their words but the intentions behind them. There were debates about misinterpreted phrases or expressions, ideas that seemed incomplete or would have benefitted from a longer conversation, and other aspects that the secondary sources felt would, in the words of one student, "never be understood by anyone but the person it happened to."

The process of collection and evaluation helped illustrate problems inherent of source analysis but also moved the class toward a deeper understanding of historiography. We reflected on how historians grapple with competing, sometimes contradictory, interpretations—the idea that historical analysis is improved by multiple perspectives and that whereas a perfect retelling of history is impossible, or at least impractical, our understanding of the past may improve through collaboration. We also broached a topic I have found to be the least-understood aspect of the historical process, the creation of appropriate historical questions. When secondary sources asked questions of primary sources, their understanding of scholarly questions and historical scholarship in general became less abstract. I asked one student what made her question worthwhile and why others would or should we care about the answer. She explained that it would help her better understand the story and that her summary would be incomplete without it.

Alternative Education 123

I closed the activity by reading Thomas Jefferson's 1802 letter to the Danbury Baptists, where he expresses a desire for "a wall of separation between Church & State." We discussed the importance of this idea, as interpreted by Supreme Court Justice Hugo Black in Everson v. Board of Education, then by lawmakers in the decades since. I asked what other information might help us better understand Jefferson's position. Students applied the logic of the sources from sources exercise and asked, "What was Jefferson's religion?" "What else did Jefferson write about the subject?" "What did his friends believe?" And, "What have other historians said about this?"[4]

The second activity, "picture chain," delivered two months later, attempted to reinforce the ideas of primary source selectivity and historical significance but also introduced the concept of change over time. Classes were again divided into groups of three to four, and each group was handed pictures corresponding to their unit on World War II. A mixed assortment of forty-five images from the 1930s and '40s depicted aspects of culture, politics, social movements, economic issues, and of course war. Each image included a date and brief one- to two-sentence caption but no information on how one image related to the next. Students were instructed to build a "chain of historical causation" by selecting five images they felt best told the story of World War II. They were to develop their groupings, title their collections, and prepare a short summary of how the images fit together. Most groups went for the images they knew best—a picture of Hitler during the Anschluss, followed by J. Howard Miller's "We Can Do It" propaganda poster, images from the landing at Normandy, the Battle of the Bulge, or the atom bomb, and images from VE or VJ Day. Some of the more creative examples included the following: a Japanese recruitment poster, a painting of a bucolic pre-war Japanese village, a photograph of a desolate, burned-out hillside on Iwo Jima, and a photograph of the devastated city of Nagasaki. Another grouping began with an image of a Chinese village destroyed during the Rape of Nanking, an anti-Semitic propaganda poster from Germany, two American political cartoons featuring racist depictions of Japanese men, and last the Norman Rockwell painting "Freedom from Want," a purified, simplistic version of the white American family.

In their discussions of historical connectedness, groups selecting well-known images discussed the war in political terms but as a series of events linked more by chronology than by cause and effect. The more creative groupings were held together by a deeper appreciation of historical significance. The aforementioned collection featuring images of pre- and post-war Japan were tied together with the title "No Peace." When asked how their pictures told the story of World War II, students responded by saying that the war was about humans and suffering and that regular people, not political leaders, die in war. "The real story of World War II," the group leader added, "is all about the little guy." Authors of the second grouping titled their collection "Hate" and connected their images with what one member observed as the "two-faced side of American history." The group agreed

124 *Creating Historical Thinking and Learning*

that World War II had everything to do with racial prejudice and "feeling like everyone was better than everyone else."

Apart from acting as historical Rorschach test, the image exercise drew out unexplored connections between content and causation. In at least a few cases, students embraced the "why" over the "how." By creating their own historical summaries, students also gained an appreciation for the scale of the conflict and the wide-ranging, seemingly limitless opportunities for research and interpretation. They learned they there is no single, perfect historical account. Moreover, and more importantly, students could reflect on how personal choice influenced the historical process. In the classroom discussion that followed the activity, I asked students to describe their attachments to certain pictures. We then discussed how individual choices of historical evidence sometimes influence larger historical arguments, how it is possible to tell different stories of the same event, and the idea that all interpretations add value to our understanding of the past.

Feeling confident with our progress, I returned a month later for the third activity, "historians in a box." Here I attempted a more advanced discussion of historiography, this time although individual schools of historical thought and with the benefit of textual sources. I delivered a short lecture on three major historiographical traditions—political, social, and cultural history—and with the assistance of the class, I examined short, paragraph-length excerpts from works conforming to one of the three traditions. I then presented the class with a bulleted list of primary sources: titles of legislative bills, pages from a ration book, names of international military conferences, letters from a U.S. soldier to his wife, the 1943 State of the Union Address, and other sources corresponding to their unit on World War II. I asked them to arrange the evidence into one of the aforementioned historiographical categories by identifying items of potential political, social, or cultural significance.

I intended to use this as a jumping-off point for a discussion of perspective, source interpretation, and the search for historical truth; the object was to have students consider the relative merits of each tradition before identifying with one. But the exercise collapsed when a brief review of the primary sources selections revealed unfamiliarity with basic content. I recovered and listed terms drawn directly from their textbooks, but this only exposed another problem. Students could identify sources of political importance but struggled to grasp why historians would select anything else—that is, how a comic strip or personal account from a Japanese internment camp could facilitate greater understanding.

I redirected the conversation to a more basic question of primary source interpretation and drew from our discussion of Jefferson's letter to the Danbury Baptists. I asked how they might classify the document's historical value, whether it had political, social, or cultural significance. Most were stumped by the question. Those who could respond believed it had political importance but could not express a rationale for their decision. I asked them to consider the document's social value and reviewed the main tenants of social history—its focus on matters of public concern, its attention to everyday life and "real people," and the ways it discusses networks or interpersonal connections. Only a few saw it as a potential source for religious history or more specifically, for a history of the Baptist Church. I hoped students would interpret the evidence in a manner fitting each theoretical position, eventually guiding them to the conclusion that theory drives the interpretation of primary sources. However, the exercise ended with a good deal of confusion and without the same impact as previous activities. Students were only slightly more aware of historical theory but now were mystified by the interpretative process.

I reassessed these same students after the last of these in-class activity sessions, and the results were encouraging. Answers to the first question, "What is the purpose of history?", were now more complex. "It tells us about our past as humans so we aren't clueless and unknowing," one student responded. "[T]o learn about people and lives that have been affected by events," another added. Historians were still simply "teachers," but responses to questions three and four, asking students to consider how different interpretations of history work together and if these interpretations change over time, showed greater levels of intellectual maturity. On the question, "Can historians have different interpretations yet be similarly correct?" students now responded with "yes, depends on perspective and, evidence," another added, "yes, because not all have the same information," and "Yes. Everybody interprets information differently." Nearly all agreed that our understanding of history changes over time and that this change is the result of new discoveries and new perspectives, not opinion.

Anecdotal evidence from Mr. Butcher confirmed these results. Students showed an increased interest in the days following each activity session and took special notice of the historians responsible for the secondary content. "Students would ask me about the author of a textbook, why we were looking at a picture, and why we were studying one topic instead of another," Butcher added. Critical awareness made slow progress over the course of the year and gave students a different expectation for their materials. "It definitely made a difference in how they thought about history. I think it improved the overall experience and made them better learners."

If anything, these limited results show that advanced historical theory may have a place in alternative education. Incorporating historiography is possible even in a crowed curriculum and among unhabituated learners. Success in these environments, however, requires instructors to maintain the same expectations they would in any program yet shift their method of delivery. Classroom activities focused on storytelling and images may help move the process in a positive direction. A distinctly non-textual approach does not seek to replace text-based sources and does not discredit or otherwise undermine the necessity for close reading or a critical evaluation of the same. Personalizing the historical process may in fact promote greater levels

126   *Creating Historical Thinking and Learning*

of interest in documents, narratives, and monographs; students come to see text as the end result of well-reasoned decisions that move us toward an understanding of, but do not "prove" the past. It is for this reason that these same methods may also have a place in the traditional curriculum, and as part of a differentiated model of instruction. The Common Core emphasizes research and the accumulation of research skills throughout the standards, asking students to "participate in shared research and writing projects" in kindergarten, to "conduct short research projects," as early as the third grade, and in the sixth grade to "research . . . a question, drawing on several sources and refocusing the inquiry when appropriate." Modeling aspects of the research process—the origin and perspective of primary sources, the selection and incorporation of secondary sources—becomes less daunting when approached, at least initially, without the benefit of text.

NOTES

1. Priscilla Rouse Carver and Peter Tice, *Alternative Schools and Programs for Public School Students at Risk of Educational Failure: 2007–2008,* U.S. Department of Education, National Center for Education Statistics (Washington, DC: GPO, 2010), 3.
2. Useful introductions to the history of alternative education in America include Edward E. Gordon and Elaine A. Gordon, *Centuries of Tutoring: A History of Alternative Education in American and Western Europe* (Lanham, MD: University Press of America, 1990); Maris A. Vinovskis, "Family and Schooling in Colonial and Nineteenth Century America," *Journal of Family History* 12:1(1987), 19–37; David Tyack and Larry Cuban, *Tinkering Toward Utopia: A Century of Public School Reform* (Cambridge, MA: Harvard University Press, 1995); Milton Gaither, *Homeschool: An American History* (New York: Palgrave Macmillan, 2008); Lawrence A. Cremin, "The Free School Movement: A Perspective," in *Alternative Schools: Ideologies, Realities, Guidelines,* ed. T.E. Deal and R.R. Nolan (Chicago: Nelson-Hall, 1978); and Statistics provided for the Alliance for Excellent Education, a Washington, DC based advocacy group. http://all4ed.org/reports-factsheets/the-high-cost-of-high-school-dropouts-what-the-nation-pays-for-inadequate-high-schools/ (accessed March 25, 2015).
3. Statistics on Michigan alternative education programs provided by the Michigan Alternative Education Organization, http://www.maeo.org/ (accessed February 3, 2015).
4. Thomas Jefferson, Letter to Danbury Baptist Association, January 1, 1802, Library of Congress. http://www.loc.gov/loc/lcib/9806/danpre.html (accessed January 23, 2015).

Afterword

As much as any area of education, history education is in a state of transition. If adopted and implemented, the Common Core literacy standards may help to improve efforts to focus on students' critical reading and writing skills. But without concurrent efforts to incorporate the findings from the scholarly literature on historical thinking into classrooms, it is likely that elementary and secondary school history teachers will continue to struggle to understand the connection between historical information and more authentic elements of the discipline. This problem is particularly likely if trends in educational Taylorism—focused on facile processes rather than substantive skills and citizenship concerns—continue without intervention or interruption.

The collaborative efforts described in this book provide a reasonable model for helping teachers and students understand the purpose and value of historical thinking. Indeed, without concrete efforts to develop historical thinking, such as through the study of historiography, there can be no real understanding of the purposes of historical inquiry. Unlike the TAH Project, the GVSU, WMU, and area high schools' collaborative efforts have not been predicated upon significant funding. Whereas money can certainly help, true collaboration has to rest on mutual interests and concerns. Indeed, one unfortunate lesson of the TAH Project is that money by itself cannot sustain collaboration. Because of the reality of nearly all high school history teachers' duties and commitments, it is primarily the obligation of collegiate history educators to initiate collaborative projects focused on historical thinking skills. However, once such efforts begin, the lessons of this book suggest that there will be many interested collaborators in the schools.

Index

alternative education 4, 6, 119–26
alternative high school teacher: Butcher, Terry 119–21, 125
alternative high schools: Barclay Hills Educational Center 4, 6, 119–20; Climax-Scotts Adult Alternative Education Program 4, 6, 119–20
American Historical Association (AHA) 12–13, 53

best practices studies 47–8, 58–60; inquiry 60–2; use in assessment 64
Bradley Commission on History in the Schools 54
Bruner, Jerome 15–16

Cohen, Elizabeth 15
College, Career, and Civic Life Framework for Social Studies State Standards (C3) 11, 61
Common Core State Standards Initiative 11, 17, 126, 127
content expectations 11, 37; *see also* curriculum standards
craft of teaching (craft approaches to teaching) 1–4, 6, 9, 20, 45; alternative education's relevance 119; historiography's relevance 81, 84; HTOY's relevance 47–8, 50–4, 58, 61–6, 69–70; TAH Program's impact on 29; university and high school collaboration's impact on 32–4, 38, 87, 94
curriculum standards 1, 11–12, 15, 17, 29, 61, 63–5, 77–8, 116,

120, 126, 127; *see also* content expectations

Danielson model 64
Delphi survey 91

educational Taylorism 1, 2, 3, 6, 9, 47–8, 53, 127
Egan, Kieran 79
evaluation 16, 22, 24, 26, 29; teacher evaluation 3, 4,45, 58, 60–6

Gardner, Howard 15
Gilder Lehrman History Teacher of the Year (HTOY) 3, 45, 47–55, 58, 60, 62, 64; teacher evaluation rubric 65–70
Gilder Lehrman HTOY Award Winners: Anderson, Michele 52, 64; Lichatin, Rosanne 49–51, 64; McAlister, Nathan 49, 50, 52, 53, 64; Mitchell, David 49, 52
Gilder Lehrman Institute of American History 3, 4, 45, 47–54, 58
global education reform movements 6, 62, 69; *see also* neo-liberal reform
Grand Valley State University (GVSU) 3–5, 25, 39, 73, 88, 94–5, 97–8, 102–4, 127

History Alive! 1, 15–20; *see also* Teachers' Curriculum Institute
historical thinking 2, 4, 6, 9, 45, 73, 127; historiography's relevance 80–1; history textbooks' connection 13–20; HTOY's relevance 50, 58–61, 67, 69;

130   *Index*

pre-service teachers' training 110, 112–13, 116–17; university and high school collaboration's impact on 34–5, 38–9, 87–8, 90, 105, 107

historical thinking scholarship: Ashby, Rosalyn 14, 21 n8; Bain, Robert 80, 85 n13; Barton, Keith 14, 21 n8; Cuban, Larry 7 n6, 64, 71 n31; Fischer, Fritz 14, 19, 21 n9, 80, 81, 83, 85 n14, 86 n25, 98, 108 n1; Fogo, Bradley 91, 95 n8; Lee, Peter 14, 21 n8, 61, 69, 70 n16, 107, 108 n6; Levstik, Linda 14, 21 n8, 59; Seixas, Peter 7 n6, 14, 21 n8, 59, 80, 85 n13; VanSledright, Bruce 7 n6, 14, 21 n8, 59, 70 n15; Westhoff, Laura 59, 81, 82, 85 n17, 85 n18, 92, 95 n12; Wineburg, Sam 8 n13, 14, 16, 21 n8, 21 n12, 35, 41 n1, 55 n5, 56 n11, 59, 61,70 n3, 70 n4, 70 n14, 80, 85 n13

instructional technology 28, 30, 34, 52, 59, 98, 103

instructional topics in history: American Civil War 25, 52, 79; American Revolution 25, 110; Chicago World's Fair (1893) 26, 29; Chinese Communism 97–8, 113, 116; Cold War 81–2, 97–8; early modern Europe 114; Gilded Age 25; Great Depression 18–19; Mao Zedong 82, 93, 111–17; modern Civil Rights Movement 82, 93, 97–8, 102–4, 106, 108; Progressive Era 25, 26, 61, 119; Roaring Twenties 18–19; Roman Republic 113–14; World War I 26, 92, 108; World War II 52, 92, 115, 123–4

International Baccalaureate Program (IB) 5, 36, 81, 89–94, 98–100, 102–3, 109, 113, 115, 117

JSTOR 94, 100

Kalamazoo Regional Educational Service Agency (KRESA) 24, 37

Kalamazoo Valley Museum 24–6
Krug, Mark M. 79, 85 n 9

literacy 11, 54, 68–9, 12021, 127

Michigan Citizenship Collaborative Curriculum (MC3) 11
Michigan Council for History Education 36, 41, 49
Michigan Department of Education 37–8

National Council for History Education 58
neo-liberal reform 6, 69; *see also* global education reform movements
No Child Left Behind (NCLB) 1, 47, 58, 62–64

Organization of American Historians (OAH) 79

Portage Central (Michigan) High School 2, 4–5, 31–40, 73, 81, 84, 87–99, 103–7, 109, 111–18; administrators and teachers: Alburtus, Eric 32–5, 90; Baker, Kent 4, 36–7, 89, 91–3, 97, 102–3; Brown, Sara 4, 5, 88–9, 91, 94, 100; Hoffman, Sue 5, 104; Johnson, Patricia 4–5, 89, 91–2, 97; Perry, Richard 33–4, 37; Salisbury, Tama 4–5, 39, 89, 91–3, 97
pre-service teachers 2, 5, 32–3, 35, 75, 82–3, 87, 90, 93, 95, 98, 102–6, 109–18
professional learning communities (PLCs) 58, 65–7

Race to the Top 58, 63
Ravitch, Diane 62, 64

social studies scholarship: Cox, C. Benjamin 77, 79, 85 n4, 85 n11; Evans, Ronald W. 70 n17, 78–9, 85 n4, 85 n6, 85 n8; Hunt, Maurice P. 76, 84 n3; Massialas, Byron G. 77, 79, 85 n4, 85 n11; Metcalf, Lawrence E. 76, 84 n3; Oliver, Donald W. 77, 85 n4; Robinson, James Harvey 75–6,

84 n1; Shaver, James P. 77, 85 n4;
Singer, Alan J. 78, 85 n7; Wesley,
Edgar Bruce 76–9, 84 n2, 85 n5;
Wronski, Stanley P. 76, 84 n2

Taylor, Frederick Winslow 18, 47
Teachers' Curriculum Institute (TCI)
1, 11–17, 19; *see also History
Alive!*

Teaching American History (TAH) Project
3, 22–32, 37–41, 52–4, 127
technology-based curricula 2, 22

value-added measurement (VAM) 63–4

Western Michigan University (WMU)
2–6, 24–5, 31–40, 73, 87–8, 94,
97–8, 109–10, 119, 127